NO, YOU SHUT UP

NO, YOU SHUT UP

SPEAKING TRUTH TO POWER AND RECLAIMING AMERICA

SYMONE D. SANDERS

HARPER

An Imprint of HarperCollins*Publishers*

HarperCollins books may be purchased for educational, business, or sales promotional use. For information, please email the Special Markets Department at SPsales@harpercollins.com.

FIRST EDITION

Designed by Kyle O'Brien

Library of Congress Cataloging-in-Publication Data has been applied for.

ISBN 978-0-06-294268-5

20 21 22 23 24   LSC   10 9 8 7 6 5 4 3 2 1

*To Averi, Daniel, Jose, Madre, and Daddy
because each of you believed I could and are a large part of
the reason I can.*

CONTENTS

NO, YOU SHUT UP

INTRODUCTION

Greetings! Let's get down to business.

Have you ever been making a really great point when someone tells you to shut up? As if you don't know what you're talking about or your point isn't valid enough? As if you did not have permission to give your opinion? As if you weren't qualified to speak on something in the first place?

Well, I have.

In August 2017, I was on air at CNN discussing the atrocities at the hands of white supremacists in Charlottesville, Virginia. What was a far-right protest against the removal of a statue of Robert E. Lee had quickly turned into a display of violent aggression against marginalized people: one counter-protester. She was killed when a neo-Nazi drove a car into the crowd, and nineteen others were injured. The CNN segment I was taking part in came after Trump's comments blaming "both sides" for the violence, though of course only one side had committed any.

I was appearing live on *New Day* on CNN with Chris Cuomo alongside Ken Cuccinelli, the former attorney general of Virginia. My argument was that what happened in Charlottesville was a gruesome manifestation of white supremacy, a problem that has grown more virulent and violent since Trump took office. Cuccinelli disagreed. He claimed the violence was an aberration, the result of an individual organizer's plot to disrupt what was billed as an innocent protest.

I was, I admit, annoyed at this rationale. These were neo-Nazis and white supremacists that had come together to inflict terror upon this community, with advance planning; this was not a peaceful, spur-of-the-moment gathering. The debate got heated, and we began talking over each other. Cuccinelli accused me of jumping from one thing to another; I replied that I was being factual, and he was hedging to avoid the heart of the issue. Cuomo jumped in to ask Cuccinelli what, exactly, he was disagreeing with. "You know what white supremacists are about," Cuomo said. "You know what Robert E. Lee evokes. That's what they use for the basis for coming to gather. What is your point of disagreement exactly?"

Cuccinelli again tried to redirect the conversation, drawing attention to "the local blogger who got the permit to protest," saying the protest was an "excuse" on his part, not a part of a larger scheme. By that point I was fuming.

"And now someone's dead," I cut in.

Cuccinelli did not like that.

"Can I finish, Symone? Will you just shut up for a minute and let me finish?"

"Pardon me, sir," I began, my voice getting louder. (He was no match for me on that front.) "You don't get to tell me to shut up on national television."

Cuomo agreed, and he said so.

"Then how do you make them stop talking when they keep interrupting you?" Cuccinelli continued.

"'Them'? 'They'?" I said. "I'm sitting right here!"

It doesn't matter what Cuccinelli looked like, how old he was, or how powerful (read: old white man politician), we all know that isn't an acceptable way to speak to anybody. And I told him so, on national television: "Under no circumstances do you get to speak to me in that manner."

YUP. He told me to *shut up on national television*. I had a right to have my voice heard, and my perspective was crucial to the conversation; however, when you're speaking truth and spitting *facts*, sometimes the powers that be try to shut you down. Well, just like I had to claim, reclaim, and assert my power on CNN that day, in the iconic spirit of

Auntie Maxine Waters (one of my heroes) . . . the time has come for all of us to band together and do the same.

We are at a pivotal moment in our nation's history. I'm not only talking about the lead-up to the next election. I'm talking about this very moment, where white supremacy is no longer being quietly tolerated or waved away, but is being actively promoted by our own elected officials. When I had my tête-à-tête with Cuch, he was just a former state attorney general. You know what he is now, as I write this? He's the Trump administration's acting director of the Citizenship and Immigration Services office. And you know what he said on Erin Burnett's show on CNN today, the day I recount that story to you? Of the inscription on the Statue of Liberty, from the iconic Emma Lazarus poem "The New Colossus"—you know, *Give me your tired, your poor, Your huddled masses yearning to breathe free / The wretched refuse of your teeming shore*—he said, "Of course that poem was referring to people coming from Europe." Not Black or brown or melanated people, of course. He spent the rest of the interview essentially advocating for policies that make our country whiter and less welcoming to diversity. This comes a few weeks after the president of the United States told four congresswomen of color to "go back" to the countries "from which they came," even though three of the four were born RIGHT HERE and the other has been a naturalized citizen since she was a teenager.

More than ever, we need to stand up, not shut up. And

so this book is for all the people who have ever been told to turn back or go quietly. I know folks want us to pipe down, wait our turn, earn our stripes. Folks want us to temper our expectations, be respectful, and just let the "seasoned adults handle things." This book is for any person who has been told they dream too big. Anybody who has been shut down, shut out, talked over, ignored, talked down to, or dismissed. This is for every single young person, and young person at heart, out there who has a passion, an idea, a spark, but the powers that be just won't let you live.

I've come to say: NOT TODAY!

So, how do we get started, you say? First off, let's not waste our time looking for a magic wand that we can wave and suddenly solve all of our country's problems. How many of you have heard the expression "If I had a magic wand, I'd . . ."? Well, guess what? I don't have one in my handbag, I can't pull one out of thin air, and you're not going to find one buried in the back pages of this book (there's some other great stuff back there, though, I promise!). So let's not wait for a fairy godmother or a magician to save the day. We don't need to wait for anyone or anything.

Also, getting started is exactly that: it involves a beginning, taking steps in the direction you want to go. Some people want to think we can just wipe the slate clean and start over, just take down the whole darn thing and create a new government from the ground up, with our designated survivor leading the way. What's that, you say? Oh, whenever all of Congress comes together for the State of the Union address, a cabinet member is picked as the designated survivor (DS); he or she is kept in an undisclosed location in case all hell breaks loose and the Capitol building gets blown up with all of our leaders inside (you know, or something like that). The DS then becomes acting president of the US.

There's actually a show on TV right now with this premise. In the first season, this new president and his team are working through the crisis, trying to figure out how it happened; they are actually presented the opportunity to rebuild democracy and do things differently. But it ain't going down like that—unless we are blowing up the Capitol, which I don't think anyone reading this book seriously wants to do (I hope to God). It doesn't work like that in reality.

What we do want is to be heard. To be taken seriously. To have the freedom to pursue our goals of a more equitable, inclusive society where everyone's future looks brighter. And to achieve that, we will not shut up. We shall not back down. We won't be quiet. The world needs us now more than ever. We are the change agents, the gurus, the masterminds, the artists, the entrepreneurs, the business folks, the politicians, the elected officials, the activists, the radical revolutionaries that we have been waiting for. IT IS US. And the time is RIGHT NOW.

Because have you seen the world lately? I mean, goodness.

1
WHO IS "WE" ANYWAY?

Before we can take on the world, or at least the political establishment, there are a few small details we need to take care of. First off, who the hell is "we" anyway? There needs to be some kind of understanding of who "we" are before we storm the gates together. Otherwise, it's going to be pretty damn difficult to work together and move forward when we get to the other side. In order to parse who "we" are, I'll give you a little history lesson, because we aren't the first to try to define a "we." Although this feels like a watershed moment in American history as far as politics and revolutionaries are concerned, it isn't the first time we've been called to bang on the gates, demanding entrance, demanding change. And demand we must. Frederick Douglass said it over 160 years ago, but it's still true today: "Power concedes nothing without a demand. It never did and it never will."

Speaking of which, *power* is something of a dirty word nowadays. But we have to address it—who has it, who doesn't, how to get it—if we want anything to change about the way our political system functions in this country. Part of gaining power comes from participation. You can sit politics out, but it is happening whether you choose to participate or not. If you don't take action and get involved at a local level, and if you don't vote in national elections, well, guess what? Someone else will. And then *they* will be the ones whose voices matter, who make the decisions that impact *your* daily life and your future.

So who is the "we" with the greatest impact on how politics happens in our country today, right now? Just start with the preamble to the Constitution. Back then, "we the people" was rich old white men. Not poor people, working-class people, women, people of color, young people. And how much has changed? Who is the "we" now?

Here's how I look at it: Think of the idea of "we" as a set of concentric circles. The closer you are to the innermost circle, the core, the more power you have—and the smaller the number of people around you. The deeper in, the more decision-making abilities you have, both as an individual and as someone who can influence politics on a local, state, and national level. Unfortunately, in our society, one of the shortest ways to increase your power is to have or make more money than everyone else. Other ways to access the core circle of power are proximity and platform. Proximity to those who are already there, or a platform that allows your opinions and ideas to matter because they can travel far and wide. On the positive side, take a look at the outsized impact of a movement like Black Lives Matter, which achieved incredible reach in a short amount of time thanks to a powerful and mobilized platform. But let's also take a look at the Koch brothers: two individuals with such enormous wealth that it allows them to directly influence national elections in an outsized way.

So again, let's go back to the "we" in the very center, the area inside the smallest circle. Here's where you'd see your billionaire one percenters and your highest level of elected officials. Here's where you'd also find the easiest access to the machine that powers the political parties— let's call it the apparatus. Step back from that inner circle into the next level, a slightly larger circle, and you'd find people like the CEOs and lobbyists and venture capitalists. Step back again: within the boundary of each circle you'll find more and more people of a greater diversity, a larger group, further from the center of power, with less and less access to the apparatus. Sometimes the borders of these circles overlap, allowing people to cross into multiple categories, like a Venn diagram. But overall, the borders are rigid. If you are in one of the larger circles, you'll have a damn hard time finding your way into a smaller one, or anywhere near the apparatus.

We need to find a way to break the boundaries that separate these concentric circles: allowing power and influence and, yes, money to flow more easily back and forth between them. I'm talking about allowing access and flow between the Dreamers, environmentalists, Silicon Valley techies, Generation Z, LGBTQ+ people, progressives, activists, Hollywood, elderly folks, Bernie bros, Southern Blacks, Muslims, labor unions, baby boomers, Latinos, moderates, the differently abled. Just to start. The largest "we," the one that contains people at the margins, needs to be able to access the power at the core.

And you know what? It's happening. The apparatus is being infiltrated. There's a generation of people, millennials and Gen Zers, those who have been influenced and bolstered by coming of age under a Black president, who feel emboldened by watching Alexandria Ocasio-Cortez, Ilhan Omar, Sharice Davids, Ayanna Pressley, and Jahana Hayes sworn into the House of Representatives. Young people's voices and ideas are being reflected in measures like the call for a Green New Deal, a visionary stimulus package that tackles climate change and income inequality, or the calls against Trump's move to "repeal and replace" the Affordable Care Act, which fell flat.

Slowly but surely, we are inching toward power. But we're talking about inches of progress. At the time I'm writing this, Alabama, Georgia, and Arkansas are passing abortion BANS. Clearly, limiting or dismantling a woman's right to control her own reproductive capacities exiles a whole hell of a lot of people—anyone with a uterus, that is—from the "we."

We must be vigilant, we must be relentless, we must be demanding. No one is going to throw open the doors to the apparatus and let us pull the levers and switch out the cogs.

Apparatus, apparatus. What is the apparatus, you ask? The apparatus is the machine that makes a political party function. For example, when folks speak about "the Democratic Party," they are really referring to the apparatus. In part it's composed of entities including, but not limited to: the Democratic National Committee, the Democratic Congressional Campaign Committee (which works to elect Democrats to the House of Representatives), the Democratic Senatorial Campaign Committee (which works to elect Democrats to the Senate), the Democratic Legislative Campaign Committee (which focuses on recruiting, supporting, and electing Democrats to positions in local government), super PACS (political action committees that can solicit unlimited donations from individuals), and the Democratic Governors Association (which provides party support to the election and reelection of Democratic gubernatorial candidates). The apparatus also contains consultants and other people who directly impact the choices we have as voters and influence who actually gets elected to office, and then, of course, the elected officials themselves.

Now, on the other side of the aisle, there is a comparable Republican Party apparatus. The major difference between the two apparatuses are the factions (constituencies, if you will) that fuel the machine, their apparatus. The Republican Party apparatus has only three factions, I would argue: conservatives, Tea Party Republicans, and Trump Republicans. If you put six conservatives in a room and ask them what conservatives believe, they will largely give you six versions of the same answer. Same thing goes for the Tea Party Republicans and for your Trump Republicans. But put six progressives, liberals, and self-identified Democrats in a room, and ask them what, respectively, progressives, liberals, or Democrats believe, and you are liable to get six different answers. Therein lies the challenge and also the opportunity when it comes to controlling the Democratic Party apparatus (because this is still about power). A wider variety of voices means more excellent ideas. It also means it can be more difficult to get people to agree and align.

You know what powers the apparatus of the Democratic Party? The different factions of people who make up the wider and wider circles of "we." We're talking about the Blue Dogs, Black women, Team Hillary, Democratic

Socialists, rural Dems, liberal baby boomers, Obama-Biden Democrats, Labor, Berniecrats, lefty millennials, the list goes on. If we took time, we could list 150 factions, I bet. All of these factions collectively power the Democratic apparatus. Some factions are happy with the way the apparatus runs, and willingly pump their energy into it. Other groups are not so happy and withhold or withdraw their efforts, possibly endangering their ability to be effective. At times, the factions may find it very hard to unite in order to change the apparatus, even if that change is for the better in the long run. But in the end, the apparatus that is the Democratic Party is nothing without the fuel—it can't function. So the question now is how the party can join its constituent parts to move forward as a collective whole.

Institutions are nothing without the people who support them; if the apparatus and the factions don't figure out how to talk to one another, the Democratic Party is destined to perpetual infighting and stagnation. Even beyond the future of the Democratic Party, the very essence of our country, the success of the American experiment, is not possible without the buy-in and participation of the people.

To date, only some factions of the "we" have enjoyed the benefits of full participation in the apparatus. In reaction to that, over the last ten to fifteen years, we've seen movements arise that I would call "apparatus adjacent."

These are movements made up of individuals and people who don't necessarily fit into a preexisting faction, and who point their criticisms at the apparatus from the outside instead of from within. It's not necessarily that these adjacent movements want to be a part of the apparatus and aren't being let in; it's that all of their goals might not be perfectly aligned with the powers that be, so they find it more powerful to agitate from the outside. At one point, the Tea Party was apparatus-adjacent; over time it's been sucked into the Republican Party apparatus as its goals became more aligned with the GOP as a whole, its ideas became more mainstream, and its leaders started winning seats. Trump Republicans were apparatus-adjacent at one point; now Donald Trump is the president of the United States of America, the head of the Republican Party, and I would largely say that his brand of politics is now representative of just another faction of the Republican Party. As Joe Biden likes to say, "This is not your grandfather's Republican Party!"

On the left there has been an emergence of apparatus-adjacent movements, like Black Lives Matter, the Women's March movement, and the Sunrise Movement to combat climate change, for example. These are all folks who don't really care to put a big D for party Democrat behind their names, because they don't see their values as perfectly aligned with the party as a whole. They work in conjunction with Democrats, and their issues align with factions of the Democratic Party at some points and in some ways, but they have not fully immersed themselves in the apparatus; they remain outside of it. I taught a class at USC last year titled "Whose Party Is It Anyway? Navigating the Democratic Party Apparatus." We went through all these really great discussions and explorations, and then at the end of the class, I said, "Okay, we've been here all semester; tell me: Whose party is it?" Immediately, students began to name different factions: Blue Dogs, blue-collar, progressive, Democratic Socialist . . . Nope. Fail. The party still belongs to the apparatus. Because the power and the influence still flow through the apparatus. So, in order to change the future of the party, we, all of the factions together, have to infiltrate it.

I learned early as a young Black girl growing up in Omaha, Nebraska, that the "we" with access to power did not seem to include me or other people like me. And wherever my pinpoint location was exactly, I knew for sure that I was way outside that innermost central circle. Accessing the apparatus seemed about as likely as making my way to Oz. But I didn't let that stop me. I'd find my way there in my Louboutins, ruby slippers be damned.

You know, when I was born, I came into this world silently—no tears. But real quick, once I found my voice, I figured out how to use it. My mother likes to say that my father took one look at me and told her, "There's going to be one set of rules for this girl, and one for the rest of the world." I guess I took his statement to heart!

My younger sister, Averi, and I were both born and raised in North Omaha. My mom still lives in the house we grew up in. (My older brother, Daniel, was born in Alaska when my parents were living out there while my dad was in the air force. And here's a fun fact: all three men in my immediate family are named Daniel. Yup, I have two brothers named Daniel, plus my dad. My dad was married once before and had a son from that marriage named Daniel Jose Sanders. Then he and my mom had their first child, a boy, Daniel Edgar II.)

In Omaha, my sister and I went to an elementary school in my predominantly African American neighborhood. Despite this, there was not a single Black teacher in our school (something that is still all too common an occurrence). After that I attended a Catholic high school, even though we were Baptist. My father said if there had been good Baptist schools, we would've gone to them, but there weren't—and my parents wanted the best educational opportunity we could have. You know what? There wasn't a single Black teacher at my high school, Mercy High School, either. In fact, some of my classmates had never even seen a person of color before meeting me and some of our classmates.

When I arrived at Mercy, a private, Catholic, all-girls

high school, I could feel myself moving closer to the next circle of "we." Well, sort of. At the end of each school day, I felt myself step back as I headed home with my sister and our friend to our Black middle-class neighborhood. I am fortunate today to not carry the burden of code switching, but as a young person, I definitely participated. As I moved between different worlds, I adapted to my environment to some degree—at times for survival and other times simply because I just wanted to fit in. Moving between different circles of "we" and then back out again is something people have to do to survive. I did it throughout my entire high school career, because I had to go to school and be able to interact with classmates and teachers, and then I had to go home and interact with my family and our neighbors. It wasn't like I was two different people, more that I was aware of the different realities and worlds that people live in. Even though my classmates and I lived in the same city and went to the same school, we lived different realities every single day, and I came to understand that early on. That said, my sister, Averi, was the one person who saw me in both environments, and she was there to call me out (and laugh at me) if she thought school Symone and home Symone were acting out of sync.

As I mentioned, there were many girls at Mercy with me who didn't know any other Black people outside the few they interacted with in our hallways. There were six or so girls of color in my grade, maybe twenty-five or thirty in the whole school of five hundred. In many respects I was your typical overachieving popular girl: I was a cheerleader, a student council member; I had lots of friends. But there was also this sense of being "other" that followed me around.

I vividly remember my parents throwing me a sixteenth birthday party, to which I invited the whole class. My family told me I could have it at the local social hall in North Omaha, and I was so excited. But the turnout was . . . a little lackluster. I had a great time anyway; people who know me know I can get a party poppin' without too much help. But still I wondered where everyone was. The following Monday in school, some girls, even a few I thought I knew well, told me, "I wanted to come, but my parents wouldn't let me go down *there*."

As the months went by, sometimes a classmate would drop me off at home after practice or a game and they'd make a joke about not feeling safe. My family lived in a regular, respectably sized three-story house; we had a yard, a porch. I realized quickly that it didn't really matter what my house looked like, or even what was actually going on inside my family or my home. External influences like TV shows or music presented my classmates with the idea that my lived experience was not their experience, or the experience of the majority of people around me—whether that was true or not. Regardless of the truth, they defaulted to this belief that I was different.

It's a sad state of affairs that in our country, in the year 2020, every Black child must suffer the rite of passage that is being called the N-word for the first time. It happened to me one afternoon when I was fifteen; I was on the track team, and a group of eight or ten of us ran this route from the school grounds to the track that took us through some residential areas. On one of these runs, a car drove by and someone yelled the N-word at me and two other Black girls. It was completely jarring for me and for all of the other girls as well, black and white. We stood there in silence, and sort of in shock. Eventually, we continued on with our run, we got to the track, we started practice. Nobody said anything because they didn't know what to say. I didn't tell my coach; no one else mentioned it either. Much later I asked myself: Why was I embarrassed? I didn't do anything. The moment wasn't necessarily this epic loss-of-innocence type of experience for me, but still it's something I won't ever forget.

The next summer, when I was sixteen, I called to ask for a job at a restaurant where a couple of my friends from school worked. The owner knew my friends and thought they did a good job, so he was like, sure, just come in and fill out the paperwork and we'll get you started. So I went into the restaurant, asked to see the manager whom I'd spoken with, and then I was told to wait. So I waited. And waited. I was there for an hour before some staff person came and told me that it turned out he was "too busy" to talk to me that day. And when I called back, they told me I didn't get the job. I remember talking to my dad, asking what I could have possibly done wrong. He reassured me that I wasn't at fault, that I'd done absolutely nothing wrong, but the larger message was one that was much harder to take.

After high school, I went on to attend a private Jesuit Catholic college, Creighton University. At eighteen I didn't know much more about my career aspirations than I did when I was ten, which was when I decided I was going to be a judge. Why? I thought judges and politicians were the most powerful people in the world. I already knew then that politicians make the laws, and judges can hold people's lives in their hands. I could see that these were the positions of real power, and I wanted to be a powerful person.

We had a mentoring program in my grade school, and the first question they asked us to answer was: If you could have a mentor in any field, who would you like to learn from? We were all raising hands, giggling and asking, "Anything? Anything at all?" They were like, anything (hey, maybe this was the start of learning to ask directly for what I want! Like when I sat in my first-ever meeting with Bernie Sanders at twenty-five years old and told him I wanted to be his press secretary . . .). I wrote down: a politician, a judge, or a chef. (A chef! HA. Anyone who knows me knows I do not cook [notice I said *do* not cook, not that I *can*not cook].)

So in seventh and eighth grade, I was assigned two mentors who were federal district court judges. Even better: they were both women! One Thursday a month, I'd get to skip school to go down to the courthouse for half a day, where I'd sit in on depositions. I kept to myself, hoping that people would forget I was there because that's when you saw the really good stuff: lawyers arguing in judges' chambers, the drama of a jury trial, all sorts of things. When the morning's work was done, the judges would take me to lunch, we'd discuss it all over a nice meal at a fancy steak house, and then they'd take me back to school. *Hell yeah, I wanna be a judge*, I thought!

All through high school, I kept in touch with these two woman judges from the mentoring program. When I went off to college, they gave me a matching quilt and pillow set for my dorm room in a very snazzy pink-and-orange patchwork (orange is my favorite color). They've both since retired, but when I recently went back to speak at the Eleanor Roosevelt Luncheon for the Douglas County Democrats in Omaha, one of them, Judge Lamberty, was there to hear my speech. Afterward, she came up and told me how proud she was!

And so, like many before me, I arrived at college thinking law school was the end goal. In fact, I figured I was going to be in Creighton's 3/3 Program, where your fourth year of undergrad is your first year of law school. You end up with a bachelor's in business and a law degree along with a master's after six years. Great. The program sounded perfect to me. I've never liked waiting. But then freshman year, they were like, "You have to take calculus." Ooooooh. Suddenly, I didn't wanna be 3/3 anymore.

I didn't quite know which academic discipline to choose, but I figured I should start trying out some career paths and work backward from there. That's how college quickly became my time of 1,001 internships. (Besides working and going to class, I also squeezed in a bit of partying here and there . . .) One of the first internships I held was at a law firm called Fraser Stryker. I still hadn't totally given up on my vision of being a judge, so I figured I should try out firm life. I applied to be a diversity scholar; some of the people at the firm had been at an event a few years prior when I had the opportunity to introduce Bill Clinton, so a few people knew who I was.

On the first day of my internship at Fraser Stryker, I walked around the office being introduced to people. Before I had a chance to say anything, person after person preempted, saying, "Where do you go to school? UNO?" Now, let me just say loud and clear, there is nothing wrong with attending a public university. UNO itself produced the likes of General Johnnie E. Wilson, a four-star general and one of only ten Black men to attain that rank. I also strongly believe that higher education needs to be made far more affordable in our country and that any young person who has the drive to attend college should be able to do so regardless of their family's economic circumstances. However, I was struck by the assumptions that people in the office were making about me, before I even had a chance to utter a word. Why was the first assumption that the lawyers in that office made about me that I must attend a state school? What other sort of implicit biases did they have about me?

As they got to know me, the comments became about how well dressed and articulate I was. People expected me to be flattered when they paid me what they thought was a compliment, but in reality, I found it confusing and embarrassing. Why wouldn't I be put together and well-spoken? Was it because I was a "diversity scholar" intern? At the firm there was one Black partner, out of a group of fifty or so attorneys; the few other Black people in the office were paralegals or interns. Did they say the same things to the other Black people working in the office, with the same underlying intonation of surprise? Did they do it intentionally, to remind me I wasn't a part of their "we" but still outside it, someone to be observed and judged by them, the ones with the real power? I let these questions float through my mind. And then I moved on. Whatever their perception was, I might never know. But I wasn't going to let it limit or stop me.

Whatever limitations I felt others might use to try and hold me back, I knew other young people had a much tougher road. In college, I got more involved in juvenile justice work, but I began my work on juvenile justice issues while still in high school, when I interned for my county commissioner, Chris Rodgers. Chris was a vocal advocate for seeking out alternatives to imprisoning young people. The first meeting he took me to changed my life. One afternoon, he invited me to come along with him to a meeting about Annie E. Casey Foundation's new pilot program, a juvenile detention alternatives initiative (JDAI) program where they were seeking out community partners for the work. The foundation was targeting a few counties across the country as test cases to see if they could reduce the number of young people in detention centers. Frankly, *detention* is just another word for *jail*, and far too many young people are automatically referred to "detention." At the meeting we met with practitioners (nonprofit program operators, school district leaders), judges, lawyers. There were three women in the room, and two Black people: me, and my boss, the commissioner. When we talked about it later, I mentioned the lack of people of color and young people present when we were discussing something that directly impacted them. Chris was like, "That's a big reason why I brought you there—I wanted you to see that. We need people like you in that room." *Damn*, I thought. *I've got some work to do.*

I saw firsthand just how few young people and people of color were involved in doing this type of advocacy work, and immediately knew that needed to change. During my sophomore year of college, I was appointed to the Nebraska Coalition for Juvenile Justice, which then led me to work with the national Coalition for Juvenile Justice (CJJ) and then the Federal Advisory Committee on Juvenile Justice (FACJJ). I realized that if I wanted to fight for the voices of young people, just showing up wasn't enough; I needed to speak up too. I applied to be the chairperson of the Emerging Leaders Committee of CJJ and won the spot. Actually, when I first got selected, the committee wasn't called that; it was called the Youth Committee. One of the first things I did as chair was change the name. "Youth" is a size on a T-shirt. It doesn't connote the type of respect we deserve.

There were plenty of well-meaning individuals on the board with me who said they wanted to hear the voices of incarcerated young people, but when I suggested that in fact we should invite them to the table, I was met with a bit of backlash (that was not something that had been done before). I remember our committee doing research to learn about young people who were doing reform work while being incarcerated. Haley Reimbold, who also sat on the committee, noted that she had the perfect person in mind— someone she met during her work with the Vera Institute. Haley was thinking of Hernan Carvente, a young man who grew up in a troubled home and was drinking by age eight, in a gang at thirteen, and the perpetrator of a violent crime at fifteen that landed him in a maximum-security juvenile jail. We sought him out and connected with him over the phone (we still chat occasionally; we're friends on Facebook). He was a thoughtful and committed advocate for himself and passionate about helping other incarcerated young people like him find a way to survive the system, and to have a chance at a future upon release. I knew right away he'd be great for our committee.

I asked for video conferencing to be set up for the next Emerging Leaders Committee meeting but didn't say why. When other board members found out it was so I could have a jailed person attend the committee meeting, I got a quiet phone call from a committee member. "Symone, we can't do this," the person said. We can't do what? "We" who? Why are we whispering? It turns out they had never had someone currently involved in the system on the committee before. But I was the chair, so I could do this. I had to fight. I know the importance of giving young people with lived experience a seat at the table. It was crazy to me that what seemed like the most obvious idea was met with skepticism. *You can't do this!* Why the hell not? Who was the "we" here? Not allowing Hernan and other youth in the system to participate in the process that was supposed to help them was absurd and exclusionary. And anyway, I was the chair. I dared someone to try and stop me from making this move. And they didn't.

Hernan joined the meeting, and he was just as prepared and passionate as I expected. Hell, you know what happened? He started attending meetings regularly (virtually). And when I stepped down from the committee, in 2015, he took over as chair when I left! Had I not argued, had I not made space, had I not questioned the assumptions about the "we" that others on the board were operating under, Hernan wouldn't have had a seat at the table. Other people with more power wouldn't have been able to see that his contributions were important. He wouldn't have joined the committee, and his valid perspective on issues that affected his daily life wouldn't have been heard. Now he's a nationally known advocate for the Youth First Initiative, a campaign working to end youth incarceration by closing youth prisons and investing in community-based alternatives.

I started off this chapter recalling Douglass's quote as a reminder that the system isn't going to change on its own. People aren't going to willingly give up power, move aside to allow us to access the apparatus. We have to first start the conversations, take steps toward moving and shifting culture, sparking and starting movements, in order to effect change in the way the political machinery operates.

When I joined the Bernie Sanders campaign in 2015, I became the youngest presidential press secretary on record. Not the youngest woman, not the youngest Black person, not the youngest Black woman. I'm telling you that, and I'm writing this book, not to say, "Look at me; I'm so special." What I actually want to say is exactly the opposite. Look at me. I'm just me, a bald Black girl from Omaha, Nebraska, with vision and ambition and a belief that I can do something important to change the state of the world. If I can infiltrate the apparatus, you can too.

I didn't grow up as part of a political legacy, or even as part of a particularly politically active family. My mother, Terri, was a seamstress early on. I call her a serial entrepreneur because she's had so many different jobs in her lifetime (guess that's where I got it from!). She owned her own sewing business, then she went to become an event planner, and then took a job with the Great Plains Black History Museum. After that she began managing a community development project in historic North Omaha, a predominantly African American neighborhood. My mother worked with the Omaha Economic Development Corporation to redevelop and reinvigorate parts of the city north of Twenty-Fourth Street. Nowadays, my mother spends her time working with the Seventy Five North Revitalization Corp where she assists the CEO. She's making a difference in her community, but politics has never been her jam.

My dad spent the bulk of his career as an engineer with the Army Corps of Engineers. Before that he was in the air force: stationed in Bellevue, Nebraska (literally down the street from Omaha), and that's how it came to be my hometown. But before that, he was just a Black kid growing up in Clarksdale, Mississippi, in the era of Jim Crow. My grandmother still lives in the house where she raised my dad; two of her other kids (my aunt and uncle) still live very close by. My dad was driven by an insatiable hunger to learn and an innate curiosity. It ended up taking him all around the world, but it always also brought him back to his faith and to his family. He was always there for the people who mattered to him, and he was unwavering in his optimistic belief that every day offered new opportunities. He refused to dwell on the hardships of the past but was always looking forward. He believed that everyone has a choice, as a person, whether to believe in and speak out about the possibility for positive change, or to get stuck in the misperceptions others might have about us, or on injustices of the past. I know these attitudes and beliefs are gifts that he passed on to me.

Though politics wasn't a focal point in my family's life, community was. My mother always took part in a lot of local activities: she would go to community meetings, she was on boards, and she is a member of Delta Sigma Theta Sorority Incorporated. She was very engaged and involved, even while raising a young family. Today she is also a member of the Links, a Black women's organization dedicated to community service. I got exposed to community work through my mother. And for us, and many other Black people in Omaha, the true center of community life was (and is) the church. On any given Sunday,

Salem Baptist Church is a place where the executives at Union Pacific sit next to the teachers and the politicians and the bus drivers, where they all come together at eight thirty a.m. and again at eleven thirty. As kids, we went to Bible study and Sunday school every week. We also went to Vacation Bible School and met a lot of people that way. In Omaha, the Black community is pretty close-knit. You get to know everybody. You don't always get along, necessarily, but you all know each other. Chris Rodgers—who was later my boss when I interned in the county commissioner's office—was also my Sunday school teacher at one point; that's how I got to know him. Same thing with the assistant to the mayor at the time, Stacy Westbrook, who ended up becoming a very good mentor of mine and is the reason I got my internship at the mayor's office when I was in college. I really credit the fact that I've come as far as I have, as fast as I have, to the community I grew up in.

PIECE OF ADVICE

RELATIONSHIPS ARE THE BUILDING BLOCKS FOR ANY KIND OF SUCCESS

I always tell people if you can go back home after it's all said and done, after you've graduated, or even during your college career and after, you should go give back. It doesn't have to be a permanent move. Just go and participate in the community that helped create and support you—or contribute to the lives of kids there who aren't being nurtured and supported. Even if your home community is well-off, there are still people (probably closer by than you think) who could benefit from your knowledge or your time or your experiences, and you can join or fund or participate in initiatives that help them.

For an entire generation of people, success meant escaping where you came from. It meant moving on and not looking back. Success was about getting out. Now it's become accepted truth that we need to find ways to invest in the communities that invested in us. Do what you can to help remove barriers to access and opportunity for others. I go home several times a year and speak to community groups or graduating classes or other gatherings. Some go home to stay or contribute to our communities by buying property or through other economic investments.

I am well aware that I would not be where I am today without the community in North Omaha. I would not be who I am. To illustrate *this, consider that the Omaha Star was the first newspaper in the country to be owned by a Black woman, Mildred D. Brown. The Omaha Star is also where I first cut my writing teeth; the editor let me have a column where I could write commentary while I was still in high school, and I continued it in college. It was the forum where I discovered that my voice could have an impact. I would go to church and people would tell me that they read my column. If I missed a week, two weeks, people would say, "Hey, Symone, what's going on? Where you been?" That would tell me that they noticed. It helped me be accountable. And that was very encouraging. I just thank God for Omaha, Nebraska, because I don't know who I would've been if I'd been born somewhere else. And you wouldn't be who you are were it not for the community that shaped you.*

As engaged as they were in other ways, my parents were not political. Yes, they voted; yes, they cared, but I wasn't raised in a house where politics was really a career option, much less a calling. I've worked alongside plenty of people who were born into political dynasties, or had activist parents growing up. I've worked alongside people with impressive degrees from Ivy League schools (don't have one of those), people with enormous incomes or inheritances (nope), many of them with egos to match (my ego might get a little bloated at times, but it always shrinks back to an appropriate size). I've sat next to world leaders and hung out with Diane von Furstenberg. I've made my way into the apparatus, and if you decide you can too, more people like you, me, WE, can work together to start to change the status quo.

In 1967, Dr. King said, "I think it is necessary for us to realize that we have moved from the era of civil rights to the era of human rights . . . [W]hen we see that there must be a radical redistribution of economic and political power, then we see that for the last twelve years we have been in a reform movement . . . That after Selma and the Voting Rights Bill, we moved into a new era, which must be an era of revolution . . . In short, we have moved into an era where we are called upon to raise certain basic questions about the whole society."

The whole society. Not factions of society, but a collective "we." After all, "we" are the everyday citizens that society doesn't work without. Who hauls the trash away from the curbs, who picks the lettuce or pulls the chickens, who works the night shift in the air traffic control tower, who rides in the back of the ambulance with the car crash victim, who works the airport security checkpoint? "We" includes people of color, along with disaffected working-class white people. Who the "we" applies to has changed over time, but the following has always been true: only some people have the full benefits of participation in society, and everyone else finds themselves marginalized, outside the circles of "we" that are closest to the apparatus and the power it contains. And WE need to change that.

2 POWER

(HINT: IT'S REALLY ABOUT INFLUENCE)

When we talk about how we can demand and create change in our country, what we're really talking about is having power. Power to control our own destinies. Power to affect the policies that our government creates and enforces. Power to ensure a livable future for ourselves and everyone else in our country and communities. Power to stand up and say: we aren't going to let people keep getting killed for their beliefs or their skin color, we aren't going to allow the planet to be trashed, we aren't going to sit down, shut up, wait our turn, wait out Trump. Power is also the ability to go on CNN wearing whatever shade of fuchsia or tangerine or turquoise I want, speaking loudly and truthfully and daring someone to tell me to shut up. I won't. We won't.

At its most basic, power is the ability to influence others, which in turn affects the outcome of events. A person can be powerful, but only because that person stands on the backs of hundreds, thousands, millions of individuals. If no one watched CNN, it wouldn't matter how informed or convincing I was when I appeared on the network as a commentator. If no one reads them, then Trump's idiotic tweets don't matter. If people don't work together to create a movement, then we can't forge a different future or course correct when things go off the rails.

Because it's only through the voices and efforts of everyone *else* that leaders have a platform they can stand on to make a difference. If we want to wield influence and lead, we have to create movements that demand to be led. Only through building coalitions and working together can we direct or influence the behavior of others and change the course of events.

Lofty goals. Where do we start? What can we do, here and now? To answer those questions, I often ask myself: Who has done it before? In our country, when we think about the civil rights movement and the leadership of Dr. Martin Luther King Jr., we think of King as a legendary, larger-than-life figure—a Nobel prize–winner, one of the most powerful and influential men in our country's history, a man who gave his life to change the world. But once upon a time, before he became the leader of a movement, he was a twenty-six-year-old preacher. He had just gotten married, just finished his PhD at Boston University. He moved back to the South for a job at a church in Montgomery, Alabama. It just so happened that within the next year and half, Brown v. Board of Education and the bus boycotts made Montgomery into a major flash point in the burgeoning civil rights movement. It was only at that point that King became deeply involved. But it wasn't until he moved south to Alabama after his time in Boston that he truly found his cause, his calling, and his followers. When he got to Montgomery, he was one twenty-six-year-old man. A year later, he was on his way to being the head of a movement.

Young people today can make a difference too. We are powerful—we are changing the world in every way, from technology to dating to music to the #MeToo movement and more. But politics, where power is centralized, is still throttled by the whims of the few—largely of an older, privileged white male majority. It's easy to feel like we have no control of our own destinies when something like the presidential election of 2016 happens the way it did. How did a man who lost the vote of the people end up holding the highest office in the land? But perhaps more alarming:

POWER

How did we end up with a bigot in the Oval Office, in the twenty-first century? To flex our power on the stage of politics, the stage where things happen that truly matter in the future of this country, we need to embrace what's unique to this generation, to use the technology, skills, and, yes, cultural mojo to make sure our voices are heard.

As a young person, I got an early firsthand view of what political power looked like. As soon as I saw it, I knew I wanted it. I was lucky enough to participate in a special organization in Omaha called Girls Inc. I like to say that I was good before I joined Girls Inc., but that program made me great. Girls Inc. was where I first got introduced to political process through the She Votes program, which teaches girls about how elections are decided and how the political process works. The board of Girls Inc. has been populated by people like Susie Buffett (yes, the Oracle of Omaha's daughter) and has hosted the likes of Stedman Graham, Malala Yousafzai, Michelle Obama, and others at their annual Lunch For The Girls fund-raising luncheon. The girls themselves serve as emcees, introducers of our special guests and hosts. In 2005, my friend Camille had the honor of giving the introduction at the annual luncheon for none other than the then senator Barack Obama. My entire life, I wanted to be just like Camille, and watching her introduce Senator Obama only upped the ante on that feeling. So when the planning began for the next year's luncheon, I lobbied the organizers that I should be the one to give the introduction to the as-yet-unnamed guest. I wasn't a natural public speaker, I'll just tell you. People often said I talked too loud, too fast, and said too much. But what I lacked in experience I made up for in enthusiasm, or so I figured.

When they announced that next year's speaker would be former president Bill Clinton, I was like, *Oh yes, I need to do this!* I told everybody I wanted to be the one to give the introduction—I told my mom, my friends, my peers. They all laughed. I told some staff and they were like, "This is a job for a public speaker"—in other words, not you, Symone. But I took it as a challenge, not a shutdown: *If you want this job, you need to demonstrate that you're a public speaker,* I decided. So, how to do that?

First stop: I went to Roberta Wilhelm, the executive director, and said I wanted to introduce Bill Clinton. "Show me," she said. *Show me you can do it. Prove to me that you have what it takes.* So I joined all of the volunteer committees I could. I inserted myself at the center of the organization, making sure they could not forget who I was. I emceed the talent show, just showed up whenever I could. I went back to Ms. Roberta and asked, again and again, almost every day.

And then I got my chance: Girls Inc. was doing a joint presentation with Camp Fire USA, and I volunteered to be one of the girls to participate. I prepared the hell out of my speech, practiced it over and over, made sure I was polished and prepared. And then, showtime. I spoke slowly, I was funny, I didn't yell or get freaked out. I took the opportunity to demonstrate that I could do the job and do it well. And I killed it. The next day when I arrived at the center, there was a message for me at the front desk that I should go to Ms. Roberta. When I got to her office, she told me that I would be the one to intro Bill Clinton at the luncheon. Now I needed to write my own speech, and the Secret Service had to vet me. I was like: *The Secret Service?!* It sounded super scary. What were they going to ask me? What if I failed some kind of top secret quiz they had? I told Ms. Roberta I was freaked out. She asked: "Have you robbed anybody lately?" "No, ma'am," I said. "Okay, then. You'll be fine."

And then suddenly it was the day of the luncheon. This was going to be the biggest moment of my life thus far, and of course I wanted my parents there to witness it. I had been very adamant to the Girls Inc. folks: "I need two tickets, one for my mom, one for my dad, two tickets." They kept telling me I could only have one, and I insisted over and over I had to have two. I had been talking about this for such a long time at home. I had practiced, I had prepared, I had read up on Clinton and was so excited. The morning of the event, it felt like a holiday since I didn't have to go to school. I got dressed and I was standing in the hallway, and I'll never forget, my dad came out, and I was like, "What time are you coming to the luncheon?" And then he told me he wasn't going. You know what he said to me? He said, "Tell Bill I said *hey*." I could not believe it. And then my dad made some sly remark, something about the economy. And I just looked at him dumbfounded. "You're not coming?" And he said, "No, I'm not going to see Bill Clinton." Oh. Oh. Okay. That was when I figured, *Oh my God, my daddy is a Republican!* That's the only way you're not coming to see your daughter have a life-changing moment introducing a former president; you must be a Republican. He could have told me he was a vampire, that's how shocked I was. He denied he was Republican when I asked, and when I asked again and again in the years after. He swore up and down that he was an independent voter. *Okay*, I decided. *I can respect that.* It fit with my dad's persona—the value he placed on knowing yourself and choosing to do what you believe is right, rather than what any leader or party says you should believe or do. That's where I get some of my nerve to be loud and strong in speaking out for what I believe in.

So I got to the venue, and I walked into the room where I was going to meet Bill Clinton. As soon as he arrived, he put me at ease. He was friendly and warm and gracious. I remember saying to him, "I've read so much about you." He shocked me by saying, "Well, I've read about you too!" Turns out the organizers had given him a packet to prep for the event that included a bio and some other details about me. He remembered them all, and he also asked me some additional questions about myself and what my aspirations were. *So, this is how it's done*, I thought to myself. *This is how an excellent politician gets you to vote for them!* They make it about YOU, and they make you feel important, like you matter as much as they do. Because after all, there wouldn't be elected leaders without an electorate.

Then we walked out onstage together. After I introduced him, Bill Clinton said, "Symone spoke so well that I hate to follow her!" In his remarks he brought up stuff I had just mentioned to him backstage. He spoke so smoothly you'd have thought he had his speech prepared weeks in advance—but then he was referring to things I had told him moments before, things he wouldn't have known except for talking to me. I realized right then and there that that's the kind of speaker I wanted to be—someone who makes people feel special and who makes everyone feel at ease by being themselves, by being a good listener, and by being natural. The road that would lead me into politics and onto CNN definitely began right then and there, in Omaha, standing next to Bill Clinton. (And as it turns out, you can look up what Bill Clinton wrote about my sixteen-year-old self on page eighty-one of his book *Giving: How Each of Us Can Change the World*.)

The luncheon was an important lesson in learning to ask for what you want and making the most of the opportunities that you are given or that you earn. Not only did I ask over and over to have the opportunity to introduce Bill Clinton, but once I actually got onstage with an audience, I found a way to talk about my goals too. It was up there for the first time that I said I wanted to go to law school and eventually be a judge, knowing that powerful and influential people who could help me do just that might be in the audience. And they were. Some individuals on the board at Fraser Stryker—a top law firm in Omaha— were there. They connected with me after the event and that's how I learned about the diversity internship position that I applied to and earned once I was in college. Along the way I realized the law wasn't for me, but I was very grateful that I had the experience. (Problems with lawyering: one, I like windows, and two, I like talking to people. When you're practicing law, you don't get windows unless you're a partner, which was too many years down the road for me to wait for sunlight. And as for talking to people, well, too much of that can get you in real trouble as a lawyer or a judge.)

Once I realized the law program wasn't for me, I had to figure out what was. What sort of degree would help me get to where I wanted to be? What sort of job experience could I gain that would help set me on the path to my goal? I took a great sociology class that made me into a sociology major for a while, and with my interest in juvenile justice I thought I'd do a minor in criminal justice policy. Then I tried out political science. Understanding the theory and practice of government, and the policies and institutions that shape people's experiences of their government. The role of the media. The politics of race and ethnicity. The philosophical ideas that we use to create a concept of a citizenry. I was blown away and realized: *This is what I should be studying; this is what I should be doing!*

It was pretty obvious to me from the start that people in politics didn't look like me. They weren't young, there weren't many women, the prominent politicians were mostly from the coasts and not from the middle of the country, and most weren't Black either. But what was also clear to me was that the true power lies in the people behind the elected official—the folks in charge of putting the message together. Pretty quickly I decided that this was what I wanted to do. I wanted to be a part of a movement. I wanted to be in a position where I could help effect real change, where I could push for a greater "we" to have access to power in this country.

One of my 1,001 internships during college was in the communications department in the office of Omaha mayor Jim Suttle. During my tenure in that office, there was an attempt to recall the mayor—some people were saying he was focusing too much on North and South Omaha, and not enough on West Omaha. In a recall, you actually have to have two elections. The first is a vote on whether the people in the municipality, state, or wherever the vote is occurring, want the recall election to even happen. If that vote is an overwhelming yes vote, then there is a second election, where folks vote whether they want the elected official removed. In other words, it's a whole thing.

So I went to volunteer on the effort to beat the recall and keep the mayor in office. This is where I met Chris Smith and Robert West of Little Smith Strategies—a firm that did polling and campaign consulting. The Suttle campaign hired them to help with turnout in North and South Omaha for the recall vote. It was a hard-fought and very close battle: in the end, 38,841 voted "NO" to the recall, and 37,198 voted "YES" to the recall. Suttle stayed in office for the remainder of his term but lost the election two years later, and a Republican took office. Still, the fight was worth it, to me. I believe he was a good mayor and deserved to finish out his term.

Following the recall campaign, Chris Smith and Robert West gave me my first real job in politics by letting me continue to work with them—I copyedited talking points, worked on clients' website content, did some copywriting; they'd take me with them while they were doing candidates' assessments, fly me around the country, and generally make me feel like a real working boss lady. But in reality, it was far from glamorous. This was local politics, and they were paying me pennies. But here's the thing: it was an invaluable experience. I worked on judges' races, mayoral races, campaigns involving candidates on Native

American reservations. I learned so much about different political contexts—the essential roles everyone can play in a campaign, from the scheduler and the rest of the advance team, to the driver, to the candidate's right-hand advisors. I got to see how different styles and personalities worked in politics, and I loved it. I realized this was what I wanted to do. Helping the best candidate to get elected was how people gained access to power. This was how individuals could truly make a difference.

I stayed on at Little Smith Strategies after graduation, but I was itching for the chance to do more in electoral politics. Again, always talk about the thing that you want! Articulate it; put it out into the world. You never know who is listening, who will be willing to help you get to where you want to be. I shared my thoughts with Chris Smith, and he put me in touch with Rebekah Caruthers—a Black woman who had also attended my university. She was the deputy campaign manager working on Chuck Hassebrook's gubernatorial campaign at the time. Chris and Robert reached out to Rebekah on my behalf to see if there might be a job for me on the campaign. I anxiously waited to hear what she had to say, so I (gently) pestered them about it. Daily. Apparently, she wanted to know if I could write. CAN I WRITE?

I went to work for the Hassebrook campaign, where I started as a communications assistant. I asked for a different title and more money, but because, you know, "experience" . . . I felt like I knew more than enough about campaigning at this point to be more than an assistant, but if that's what it was going to take for me to get in the door this time, fine. Nothing lasts forever, and I knew I would prove my worth in a short time. So I said okay to the assistant title, but I also negotiated the opportunity to revisit both title and salary in a few months "pending my performance." (You don't always get what you want *the first time* you ask.) Three months later, I was promoted to deputy communications director for the campaign. It was a big job, and I loved it: I worked with our consultants, I helped scout talent and locations for ad shoots, I wrote talking points and helped prep the candidate for interviews, I offered to drive him to events (you learn A LOT when you're in a car with someone . . .), and I managed our "letters to the editor" program across Nebraska's ninety-three counties. While I was there I was honored as the youngest recipient to ever receive the *Midlands Business Journal*'s 40 Under 40 Award, given to top entrepreneurs, executives, and professionals under the age of forty.

During that campaign experience, I fell in love with political communications. You know why? Controlling the messaging of a campaign or a movement is the true source of power, and it's also fun. In the end, politics is just a bunch of messages strung together, and communications means that you put it together in a way that makes sense, in a way that tells a story, in a way that makes a case for your candidate and makes people believe in him or her.

When people say they don't like politicians, or the campaign slogans or messages don't resonate, they are saying the stories these politicians are choosing to tell aren't hitting home with the audience. Maybe they aren't keeping up enough with issues as they evolve; maybe they aren't choosing stories to share that are relevant to the particular group of people they are trying to reach; maybe their tone or their timing is off.

Here's the thing. Every campaign, whether the campaign is for county commissioner, mayor, or president of the United States, has a "theory of the case." In the law, the theory of the case refers to a succinct statement that a lawyer comes up with that encapsulates the issue to be argued and decided, the evidence that will be brought to bear, and the position of the attorney. Campaigns must have a similar animating theme, a sort of central tenet. And guess how that theory of the case is formed? Your top communications people and strategists come together in a room with the candidate and talk. And talk. And talk. And together they craft that central message that will shape everything else the candidate says and does. For Bernie Sanders, the theory of the case in 2016 was: "We live in a rigged economy kept in place by a system of corrupt campaign finance." Every policy idea he had, every other statement he made in his campaign, linked back to that central tenet of his campaign.

For Joe Biden, the theory of the case is: "Restoring the soul of the nation, rebuilding the backbone of the country, and uniting America." The "soul of the nation" part of the message speaks to combating hate and dealing with the rise of white supremacy. The "backbone of the country" refers to his focus on working people, on creating more and better jobs for the middle class, on a health-care system that people can afford, on an educational system that doesn't cripple students with debt. "Uniting America" means reasserting how we present ourselves on the world stage, how we deal with foreign policy, recognizing that America is still the greatest democracy in the history of the world. How did we get to this theory of the case for Biden? A bunch of people sat in a room talking with the candidate.

Sometimes you don't get it right the first time. Maybe people don't understand what your theory of the case is; maybe it's too abstract, maybe it doesn't speak to them, or maybe they feel it shows you don't know who THEY (the voters) are. So, back into the room the comms people and strategists go. Messages have to be authentic and organic to the campaign. When you start pandering, that's when people start to say your message doesn't resonate.

The Democratic Party apparatus has a huge communications problem. We have to fix it if we want to connect with people across many different factions and get them to vote. It is part of what cost us the last presidential election, and we can't allow it to continue to hobble us going forward. The heart of the problem is that there are so many factions within the Democratic Party, from Berniecrats to Blue Dogs to progressives to semi-Socialists. The party is composed of many people who believe and want many different things, making for a disjointed and sometimes chaotic coalition. We need to alter the Democratic apparatus (first by allowing more people access to that apparatus, as we talked about) so that it can communicate across the factions of the Democratic Party more effectively. We need to rejoin the constituent parts to move forward as a united and collective whole. And to do that, we need better communications within the factions of the Democratic Party and better messaging, more nuanced and tailored, coming out of the party as a whole.

As I write this, there are no fewer than twenty-three confirmed candidates looking for the Democratic presidential nomination—a sort of something-for-everyone buffet of personalities.

Here's the frustration that I'm hearing from people I meet with on the campaign trail and in my daily life: the Democratic Party is too concerned with telling the American people how they can make America better before focusing on what the people themselves are actually saying. The Democratic Party apparatus tells folks it will help them, that it knows best, and that it has the answers, based on how things have always run in the past. But the American people, and more specifically, the many diverse factions of the Democratic Party, are tired of this. Americans from different income brackets and age groups, religions, ethnicities, and races have all concluded that they no longer want to hear empty promises. Even people who have long been okay with how the Democratic Party has functioned in the past are fed up with the lack of forward progress. They want to see their fellow Americans speaking, and the leaders of the Democratic Party listening: they want to see Parkland students giving speeches on gun control, and congressmen and -women taking action.

When I was a fellow at Harvard's Institute of Politics at the Kennedy School in 2018, I asked my students how they would describe the current state of the Democratic Party. "Leaderless, shit show, nihilistic, eating its young, directionless, reactive, old, nationally focused, growing, cautious, damaged, dysfunctional, fractured, complacent, boring, coastal—broken." Goodness. But that's when I told them to take a step back and reminded them that when we talk about "the party" in this way, what we are really talking about is the apparatus—the DNC, DCCC, elected officials, DLCC, super PACs, DGA, consultants, and donors . . . the cogs and gears. But the factions are the fuel that powers the machine. Black Lives Matter activists, Dreamers, and pro- ponents of the Green New Deal have shifted the conver- sation in the Democratic Party—these factions are driving the Democratic apparatus forward, making the machine go, and moving it in a different direction.

The wants of the people, not the promises of party lead- ers, need to lead the way toward the future. If the party truly makes an effort to give a voice to the people, the fac- tions will not work against the apparatus in Washington, DC, but with it. If the apparatus stops telling people what they need and instead allows the people themselves to con- struct the party's messaging and directives, I believe we have a chance to regain the power and ensure the continu- ing future of the Democratic Party in this country.

Don't get me wrong, the factions are the future, but we still need strong leaders. The American people should be involved in the messaging of the Democratic Party, yes, but we still need a candidate and a president that we can vest our trust in—let's not forget this is the primary function of a democratic republic. When I ask people what that leader should look like, who that leader needs to be, the young people and the LGBT people and the people of color and the working-class people and the new immigrants and others tell me they want—WE want—somebody who is authentic, with real stories and real heart. Someone who has a vision, who is looking to create an America that in- cludes all the factions, someone who listens to the "we" and who allows their voices to be heard. What we truly need right now is a visionary, and someone with a diverse and experienced team, so that the American people can see themselves in and trust the president's entourage. Most of all, the American people want to see more people in politics who honestly, authentically, and genuinely give a damn. And the only way for this to happen is for candidates to communicate their authenticity effectively, so we can decide who has it and who doesn't. Who really means what they're saying.

When I worked on Bernie Sanders's campaign, one of the things I was most proud of was helping him communicate his authenticity. No one could argue he isn't an authentic person and leader; I mean, he has been saying the same thing for forty years. But his ability to convey that was, oh, challenged, let's say, at the time I joined his campaign. When I signed on as his national press secretary, activists from the Black Lives Matter movement were rushing the stage at his events, disrupting his speeches.

Disruption is an effective tool, and at its core it is about attention. The lack of attention paid to activists in 2016, specifically to the issues the Black Lives Matter movement raises, created an environment ripe for disruption. When I was hired, I decided to make it my personal mission to find a way to communicate the issues fueling that disruption to Senator Sanders and the other people on his campaign team in a productive manner. In addition to my duties as a press secretary, my first task as part of the team was creating a dialogue with the groups using his events to gain attention. In every single place that we had a rally for the next few months, I would get in touch with the local BLM folks and invite them to a listening session. I would tell them that the listening session would take place after the event, and if the activists ended up disrupting the events, we weren't going to meet with them.

It worked. The disruptions ceased to exist. Senator Sanders went to a lot of listening sessions during that time period that helped inform a number of policy issues that we ended up putting in our platform. BLM folks got their voices heard in a more productive and convincing manner than shouting at Bernie from the crowd, and Bernie got a chance to sit down with them one-on-one and hear them out from a place of mutual respect.

Let me be very clear, I know when I was hired to work on Senator Sanders's campaign I was often referred to as a Black Lives Matter activist (LOL). I'm proud of my involvement with the movement, but I am not an activist. I like to say I just played one on TV. My activism work has not included physically putting my body on the line; that is just not how I've contributed. I know DeRay Mckesson, Brittany Packnett Cunningham, Tef Poe, and many others; they are the real activists. They are the people who have put their bodies on the line, who have been teargassed and hit with rubber bullets because they dared to raise their voices. Now, that's authenticity. My activism looks a bit different.

While BLM is often portrayed in the media as a single, centralized movement, in reality the movement is made up of a variety of different groups with similar goals. The hashtag itself, #BlackLivesMatter, started circulating on social media in 2013, after George Zimmerman was acquitted in the February 2012 shooting death of Trayvon Martin. Then, in 2014, when Michael Brown was shot in Ferguson, Missouri, local folks organized street protests and utilized social media to tell the real story of what was happening. America started paying attention. Today there are several groups: Black Lives Matter, the Movement for Black Lives, and Campaign Zero, to name a few, all working on issues of violence against Black communities in the United States. Even though the movement is fractured, there is still important work being done in various spaces and places. I feel like part of my job is to keep these issues involved in the more mainstream political conversation, in whatever way I can. Because these issues continue to matter to me personally, no matter where I find myself in my career.

Some issues are big enough that they shape us as people. But sometimes we may also feel like we have to pretend to be someone we're not in order to own our power. And you know what? Faking it until you make it is sometimes okay. I don't mean selling out or posing; I mean channeling your ambitions. Beyoncé, after all, has her badass alter ego, Sasha Fierce. As a kid, I didn't watch a lot of TV, but every night my family watched the local news. So I knew that one of the surest ways to get people to listen to you was to be a commentator or a newscaster. That's when I invented "Donna Burns," a television journalist who used sticks, hairbrushes, whatever I could get my hands on for a fake microphone. I "interviewed" my playground friends, my family members, anyone who I could get to participate. Obviously, this memory was a big source of amusement to my family once I became a pundit in real life, on CNN on a daily basis, from September 2016 to April 2018, when I served as a political commentator.

Things have changed a lot in the media environment, especially in the past ten years, and there's a whole new system by which people gain influence and spread messages these days. Particularly now, as commentators and analysts occupy an increasingly large share of the space on cable news, being in front of a TV camera is a powerful place to be. It is also slightly terrifying to consider that there are no rules for the pundit class . . . networks are not "demanding" you tell the truth. When a booker calls you up to see if you'll be on a show they ask, *Are you available? Are you cool with these topics?* Not *Are you going to tell the truth?* There's no clause in your contract that says, *I swear to tell the truth on air.* That's why it's so important that people are there in the room and on the air with the facts, and the backbone, to call out misinformation when they hear it. More than ever, we need commentators, reporters, journalists, producers, TV and entertainment executives who care about keeping the bar high when it comes to telling the truth. We're living in a moment when some people have allowed the truth to go by the wayside in pursuit of something else (viewers . . . votes . . .), and it's a scary time.

And as I was talking about earlier, no one is going to hand you power or open the door for you to voice your opinion or your desires. You have to demand it. And part of the way you do that is saying out loud, to anyone who will listen, what it is that you want, and then backing those words up with actions. (Also, you never know who is pretending like they aren't listening but truly is.)

Don't be shy about your goals. I'm a true believer in not only speaking up but also writing down what you want—in your phone or notebook, on a scrap of paper from the bottom of your purse. Thinking about it is too abstract sometimes. So write it down, then practice saying it out loud. Then say it out loud in front of people you know, and then as you get more comfortable, in front of those you don't. It's like me saying, "One day I wanna be White House press secretary!" There. I said it. Everyone says don't tell people your dreams because it'll kill them. No! You have to express them—you have to give them oxygen in order to let them breathe and grow and become something real. They're not real if you've never told anyone about them!

PIECE OF ADVICE

WRITE DOWN YOUR GOALS AND HOLD YOURSELF ACCOUNTABLE

One of the ways to help your aspirations become reality is to write down actionable steps that will take you in the direction of your dreams. For a long time, I've kept a life outline on my phone; I don't like calling it that, but it's what it truly is. I keep it in the Notes app.

In that outline, I've always got a running list of what I want to accomplish this year; I've also got a list of what I want to do before I turn thirty and thirty-five. I started doing this in college, when it was what I wanted to do before I was twenty, twenty-five, and I wrote down stuff like: Intern in China. Get published by an international news agency. But guess what—I did them. In the winter before my second semester of senior year, I interned for the lifestyle magazine company That's Beijing, *via a program* called CRCC Asia. I was freezing in China, but it was an amazing experience. And I was published in the January 2013 issue of the magazine!

When I wrote those goals down, I didn't know how I'd get there, but I knew I wanted to. Early on, I also wrote down that I wanted to work in politics—I was telling people I wanted to work a presidential cycle, and they'd laugh and say, "You and everyone else in DC." Hey, look at me now! Getting on cable news as a regular commentator was another thing I wrote down. I knew I'd get there, but I didn't think I'd get there SO SOON!

Your dreams can be open-ended, but it's up to you to figure out the details along the way. Part of being prepared is being serious about what it is you want, and then giving yourself room to fill in the blanks. Notice I didn't say I wanted to be press secretary for a specific person in the White House. I'll figure out those pieces as I go along and when I get there. My life outline also holds me accountable: for instance, if I get an opportunity to host a game show, well, that sounds nice, but it doesn't have anything to do with my plan for my life. It doesn't fill in any of the blanks that are going to get me to my true destination. But, hey, if The View *calls*, that's something different. That's on my path—in a different direction maybe, but with the same destination.

If you're a pen-and-paper kind of person, write down five things you want to accomplish by the end of this year. Now write five things you want to accomplish in the next five years. Here's the next step, and it's important: find someone whose opinion matters to you. Could be your best friend, your grandmother, a former teacher. It doesn't have to be someone you talk to frequently, but it has to be someone who sparked the ambition in you that set you in the direction of one of these goals. Tell that person what you want to achieve, and why you connect them with that goal. It doesn't matter how you contact them: call, text, tag them in a photo of the two of you together and include this information in the comments. If you're a social media person and you're brave, maybe make your entire two lists visible to your friends, or to a select group of people. Ask people to check in with you periodically about whether you've made progress. Ask them to share their own aspirations with you.

Here's another thing about power. Sometimes you have to grow into it. So yes, I got on cable news far more quickly than I expected. But that doesn't mean my entrée to TV was a smooth ride. In fact, my first appearance on a major news network felt more like a slow-motion disaster. It was January of 2016, in the lead up to the South Carolina primary; I'd been on the Sanders campaign for about five months when I was invited to be on MSNBC with Melissa Harris-Perry. Al Sharpton was a guest, along with Alicia Garza of #BlackLivesMatter and a few other people. When I got my turn to speak, I was breathing really heavy. I was worried that it would be obvious that I was, like, panting on national TV. (Thank God you can't actually hear it, but you can see it! Look up the clips and you can literally see my chest rising and falling like I'm about to hyperventilate.)

MHP started off with a softball question about whether Bernie's campaign was "going negative," since Clinton had started tossing some barbs in our direction. I went at it, spooling out stats and referencing the Trans-Pacific Partnership, the Keystone Pipeline, national security, education, and, and . . . MHP jumped in to save me. "Damn, girl." She turned to Sharpton and, talking to us both, said, "That is what you were supposed to do on a cable TV show." She went on to say, "I'm not kidding, you're actually good at your job, right, in the role that she's in right now, you take that mic and you go, right?" Hell yeah. I wasn't polished, but I was prepared. A little later, Al said, "Symone, you're doing a great job, I wish I had you when I ran." It was funny because they were coaching me about doing TV WHILE I WAS ON TV, but I didn't care. I appreciated their support, and it was nice to hear out loud that I was doing okay.

To be honest, it got a lot easier fairly quickly as I realized that I was playing a role, as a spokesperson for Senator Sanders's campaign—I repped him. While that came with its own responsibility of representing him effectively and accurately, what made me more nervous were those moments where I was the spokesperson for *me*, saying what I want to say, what I believe in. It's so much easier to do talking points and stay on message when there is a message to fall back on; it's a lot harder when I'm sitting there on CNN or the Sunday shows and people are asking for my personal perspective on hot-button issues, asking me to weigh in or give quotes or stats. There's not only the pressure of getting the story straight, there's the added dimension of being a WOC, and a spokesperson for the culture. I want to be doubly and triply sure I'm on point, because someone out there is going to use my behavior or performance as representative for other people, as unfair as that may be. That's the way it is in our world for now, and I can't move through life, especially public life, pretending it isn't so.

For instance, in November 2018 I was on CNN's Sunday-morning State of the Union show; Rick Santorum was also there. The issue of the recent recall of romaine lettuce came up. The lettuce was contaminated by *E. coli* bacteria, and several people had died after eating it. The recall was big and messy and cumbersome, and I brought up how the FDA had killed a rule that resulted in making regulation laxer for produce before the outbreak happened. What had been a political move was now endangering people's lives. Rick Santorum waved me off and said I didn't know what I was talking about. He literally shut me down, said I was wrong, and closed the conversation. Of course, I was right about the poopy lettuce. The next day, Valerie Jarrett tweeted on how the FDA behaved irresponsibly and caused the lettuce debacle. I'd been automatically dismissed in a way that other people wouldn't. Another time I was on with Santorum, he made a factually incorrect statement, and when I called him out on it, he literally put his hand up in my face and said, "I'm not done." He refused to look at me as he gazed around at the rest of the panel. Behavior like this is not okay! And it's only going to change if people speak up and make their voices heard. I always have to have my facts because people will assume I don't know what I'm talking about. So I have to make damn sure that I do.

When you're working on a campaign, keeping your facts straight is a bit easier because there's someone who is aggregating news clips for you all the time on the most important issues of the moment. I get email blasts with regular updates, plus tip sheets and newsletters from reporters at places like Politico, the *Washington Post*, the Intercept, etc. But when it's you commenting on the news of the day from your own perspective, there is no team to make sure you are informed, and there isn't anyone writing your talking points. There is just you, your thoughts, and the foresight to read up on the headlines and regularly check Twitter so one is not caught slipping on the latest news. The stakes are super high with social media's twenty-four-hour news cycle—any gaffe will live in infamy. Even statements that aren't mistakes are spun and spat out and used against people. On the weekend in May 2019 when Biden had his first rally in Philadelphia, officially announcing the launch of his candidacy for the presidency, I was asked about the crime bill that he took part in passing during the Clinton administration, and whether I believed it led to mass incarceration. It was supposed to be a soft interview, a minute of airtime on all the positive things that Biden was about to talk about in his launch speech, a rah-rah, uplifting little segment. Instead, CNN's Victor Blackwell caught me off guard, on live TV, asking me to account for a bill that passed when I was four years old, on a subject that's super important to me, framed in a way that was, shall we say, not too kind. But the reality was, I was back on the field and no longer in the press box just talking about "the game." I was so used to being a commentator,

I forgot how to be a well-prepared spokesperson. It was a great reminder that you always have to plan ahead and prepare, and to anticipate the unexpected. I had gotten complacent, and now I was jumping into very different waters. I didn't exactly drown at that moment on CNN that day, but there was some flailing involved, the kind of splashing and thrashing around that I promised myself I wouldn't do again!

I decided to get involved in Biden's campaign in the first place because I believe we are living in dangerous times. We can't talk about power without talking about the abuse of power, something the current administration knows a thing or two about. This is what happens when enough of us "sit this one out" (election 2016) or don't pay enough attention or don't get engaged in the political process, thereby allowing other people to step in and take our place in our absence and to speak up in our silence: we end up with a situation where a certain "we" elects an individual who abuses the system, who makes a mockery of our democratic process, who divides the nation and sullies our reputation abroad. One person can truly make a difference, for good or for bad—but their ability to do so still comes down to influence.

One of the first times I spoke with Joe Biden one thing he said really struck me. He said his parents instilled one strong thing in him: when you see an abuse of power, it's your obligation to stand up and combat it. He said that was the real, underlying, and undeniable reason he knew he needed to run for president in 2020. What he's seeing from Donald Trump, what he's seeing from this administration—from children in cages to the rampant abuse of power from everywhere, from the Department of the Treasury on down—is, one, not who we are as a nation, but, two, is a direct affront to his, Joe Biden's, personal values. And I felt that to my core. And I was like, *You know what? I think this is where I want to be.*

Because if power is really about influence, there's truly no more powerful place to be than in politics. Whether we like it or not, the current bipartisan political system in the United States of America is not changing in a drastic way any time soon. The group of people who create the laws, the people who make decisions on a local, state, and national level about how this country should run, who make judgments about whose voices are heard and whose needs and interests are given priority and attention, is a question of politics. Power concedes nothing without a demand. If we want the apparatus to change, we have to go in there and change it ourselves. Some people say they don't believe that real progress can come about in this way. They want to say, we don't want a seat at the table, we want to topple the table, smash it right down the middle, watch all the fine china and silver crash to the floor. But tell me how that's really going to work out. If you burned everything to the ground, if we suddenly decided to abandon or overthrow our current system of government, lots of people would die. Forget running out of organic kale. Ambulances would run out of gas. The taps wouldn't turn on. Trash would pile up. Chaos and disorder and sanitation disasters left and right.

Instead, we have to be thinking about how we want to do things differently: How can we bring a sweeping change into a system that does not want it or allow for it? The "we" who runs the apparatus is going to tell you no at every turn. So how do we claim power for ourselves?

Movements have power because they wield influence. So to claim our power we have to assert our influence—but that doesn't just happen. It must be built. Unfortunately, sometimes attention for a cause, and thereby the degree of influence of those rallying around it, is galvanized by great tragedy. The Black Lives Matter movement was born out of Trayvon Martin's death, and Tamir Rice's death, and the deaths of so many other innocent young Black people by the hands of police in our nation. Or the outpouring of support for new measures of gun control, necessarily growing in size and power after horrific incidents like Sandy Hook and Parkland. Activists rally around injustices; movements gain a stronger voice and make demands that are actually heard, rather than ignored. When more people join the chorus, when enough voices cry out and leaders hear them and help take up the cause, that's when big change really starts to happen.

And then, when you finally have their attention, it's not enough to demand just a few incremental changes and say, "Okay! We're good!" or to feel satisfied by the small victories. Criminal justice reform is a recent example—people are still getting locked up for marijuana possession in some places, while in others their fellow citizens are making bank off of legal sales of the same thing. We haven't solved the underlying issues of inequality, of people being treated differently by the justice system depending on their income or their race. The tendency is that when we get a little bit of change, people start saying, "WOW! This is what we've been working for! Good for us!"

Why do people like to coast on small victories? What is the appeal of making them out to be a grand win? Well, for one, the president can be like, "I threw a bone to minority communities," and the next time someone says he has a racially insensitive policy or program or is trafficking in straight-up racism, or suggests the administration is blocking civil rights progress, he can shrug his shoulders and not get beaten up for it. But we always need to ask: What are the next steps? How can we keep pushing forward? I don't work for incremental change. Yes, I understand change takes time. Sure, I'm going to celebrate the small wins—but then I'm going to get up and go back to work the next day. Please come with me.

3 REDEFINING NORMAL

(OR: *WHY BE NORMAL WHEN YOU CAN BE FABULOUS?*)

We the people—young people, women, people of color, differently abled, nonbinary—do not always get to set the terms of our existence. So much of what we are able to do—the types of jobs we are considered for, the maximum income we can attain, the highest levels of power we can achieve, the places we are expected to live, and how we are supposed to spend our time and money—is confined by the expectations of society, by precedents that were set long ago and have been maintained over our country's history by those who wish to stay in power. By design, our presence is felt to be "out of the ordinary" in many circumstances. It's not "normal" for us to show up in certain places, like an elected position or the corner office. *We* are often made to feel like we aren't, in fact, "normal" at all. We're different; we're the "other." We're told we have the wrong name, the wrong color skin, the wrong religious beliefs, the wrong body type. That we're too "out there" to be taken seriously in politics. Too loud for cable TV. Too young for power.

Black boys and girls are still being killed at the hands of police, folks coming to this country for better lives are still being deprived of citizenship, women's reproductive rights are being curtailed and denied. We are still demeaned in the workplace, refused privileges enjoyed by others; we are still fighting for equity in this nation. Activists are organizing to stop gun violence, lobbying to remedy the fractured criminal justice system, decrying the economic inequality that feeds the huge gulf of opportunity between the rich and the rest. Sixty-six percent of young Americans have more fear than hope concerning the future of this nation. Half of young Americans believe the American dream is dead. Seventy-five percent of young Americans have very little trust in the government.* Folks want out with the old and in with the

---

*Harvard Institute of Politics, Spring 2018 Youth Poll, April 2018, https://iop.harvard.edu/spring-2018-poll.

new: they want to see new topics being discussed in the Democratic Party, new people taking leadership roles, and, most important, concrete action to follow these deliberations.

To start taking steps in this direction, I've come to the conclusion that together we need to reject the concept of normalcy. Normalcy is the very concept that empowers purveyors of racism, sexism, and white supremacist ideology. How can one set out to do the things that haven't been done before, to shift power dynamics, if we are concerned with being "normal"? "Normal" is the status quo—ignorance of the needs of the entire "we." Instead, WE want to be acknowledged, appreciated, recognized. To be able to make a difference in our communities and in our country: that is what we should truly aspire to. To discard any previous definition of "normal" and make our own.

I sure as hell didn't grow up aspiring to be normal. I don't want to ask permission to exist or for entrance to any group of people. I know that won't get me anywhere, or surely not at the rate of speed that I consider acceptable. I take to heart what the ancient leader Hannibal, one of the greatest strategists of all time, said: "I will either find a way, or make one." No one is standing at the door to the apparatus saying, "Welcome, person that has been locked out of opportunity for decades! Let us help you find your footing." So how do we find a way in? How do we make a path for ourselves when no such trail exists?

First of all, we need to be prepared to hear "no" at every turn. We need to be prepared for struggle. We need to know that the changes we make might not feel good at first, certainly not to everyone involved. The system will still be in place—some system always will be. Change-making work doesn't mean you get to just toss out the system, the apparatus, and install something new. We have to take the system we have, which thankfully is a somewhat flexible and open system, our democratic republic, and change it to make it work for us. To do that, we need to allow everyone to play a role, depending on their strengths and how comfortable they are being on the front lines of change. As individuals, I would say that also goes hand in hand with knowing your boundaries. Be prepared to have them questioned. Know how you are going to act and re-act when a cause or a person or a candidate pushes you to the limit of your moral or ethical beliefs. I'll go into that in more detail in the next chapter.

But first, I know a thing or two about being told "no." Right before I went to work for the Sanders campaign, I was told no twenty-seven times—and that was just in one season of job interviews. I knew that I wanted to work in politics after my experience with my 1,001 college intern-ships. In late fall 2014, the day after we lost the guberna-torial race in Nebraska, I packed up my stuff, and I got on the road to Washington, DC.

My first DC job was working for a consumer advocacy think tank. I wasn't super into the idea of working on trade policy, which was the focus of the organization, but when I interviewed for a job that I really wanted, to be the press person on house financial services working for Maxine Waters, I didn't get it. The interview went well, though, which was encouraging—they said they really liked me but that I needed technical writing experience. So I thought, *Fine, I can do that.* I started to look around and found something at Public Citizen's Global Trade Watch. It doesn't get more technical than America's trade policy! I knew nothing about trade, but dammit, if that's what it was going to take to get me in the door to my next stop in politics, I would learn about trade policy. My boss was super tough—everything I wrote, she would send back dripping with so much red ink it looked like blood. The topics weren't ones that I came to most naturally. But I learned a lot there, including about Senator Sanders, who was deeply invested in these issues of economic equality. And so I learned the issues, I took what I could from the experience, and six months later, I knew I wanted to move on to a job in *politics*-politics; I didn't love issue-based advocacy work. So I started going on interviews . . . a lot of interviews.

If there was a Democratic entity in Washington, I interviewed there. I prepped for, dressed up for, showed up to, and sat through twenty-seven interviews. The DCCC (Democratic Congressional Campaign Committee) put me through eight rounds of interviews only to decide not to hire me (the position was for speechwriter for the chair of the organization). They said I was "Really nice! A joy to have in the office!" I present so well! But they were "promoting internally." WHAT! Why did they keep calling me back? Oh, and the parting words: "We'll keep you in mind for campaigns when we're hiring for fall." Damn. I really had a moment of reckoning at that point: Am I not going to get a job in politics? Should I start thinking about some other career path, where I fit the mold of *normal*? I applied for a communications job at an energy company, I looked at doing fund-raising, I thought about going to work in corporate communications or at a public affairs firm. A good friend of mine had just gotten a job at Deloitte. "Come work with me!" she said. "You'll totally get a job if you apply." I thought about it. I decided maybe I should. I waffled. The money was great, the work was reliable and predictable, and I'd be good at it. I talked to them, and they said they'd hire me, but I knew it wasn't what I truly wanted—I wanted to work in politics, where I felt like I could truly make a difference while also doing work I found personally rewarding.

Then one day, while I was still at work at the trade organization, I got a random call from someone named Jeff Weaver. He introduced himself as Bernie Sanders's campaign manager. He told me he'd gotten my résumé from someone whose name I didn't even recognize. (Eventually

I learned Jeff had gotten my résumé from the former campaign manager of the governor's race I'd worked on in 2014. It just goes to show that you have no idea where the critical connection will come from, so impress everyone!) Would I consider coming to work for Bernie Sanders? Jeff asked me. At this point I got up and shut the door to my office. "Tell me more," I said.

Two days later, I was on my way to Senator Sanders's office. I met Jeff, and we had a good rapport right away. He said: "We need help. I really like your résumé." Jeff told me, "We're struggling with some of our messaging. We need someone like you on board." At the end of it, I thought, *I like him, he likes me*, but there was nothing really official said.

Two weeks later, I heard from the senator's communications director. We agreed to meet up at a restaurant. When I sat down, he had two phones on the table and they both kept going off, one after the other, back and forth. It was pretty immediately clear to me: they needed help. We started talking about issues like trade, the economy, and criminal justice reform. The communications director commented that he thought I would be really good talking about these issues on the radio. "Hmm, well," I quickly retorted, "I would be good at talking about these issues to actual reporters as well as on television if need be."

Another two weeks went by. Now it was June 2015. Another week. Crickets. So I was like, *Cool, I've had twenty-nine interviews now . . . and I still don't have a new job.*

In the midst of all this, Netroots Nation—a major annual progressive political conference—happened. The 2015 conference took place right after the death of Sandra Bland, a twenty-eight-year-old Black woman who was pulled over for failing to put on her turn signal when changing lanes: three days later, she ended up dead in her jail cell while in police custody. As Senator Sanders was addressing the conference, activists started interrupting him by calling out the names of Bland and other Black people killed in recent years by the police. Needless to say, the encounter did not go well; Bernie looked flustered and out of touch, and the videos and coverage went viral. I saw this and thought: *Okay. Maybe I don't want to work for him anyway, because perhaps he has a Black problem.* But a nagging voice in my head also said, *Maybe you should go to work for him, because his message is important. And he might not actually have a Black people problem.* His larger vision was important, and I believed in it. I also believed in the value of having the voices of the activists heard.

Had they not called me, I would not have pursued the job further. Here's why: it is important to me that I am working for and with people who have a level of cultural competency where people of color, especially Black people, are concerned. So when watching Bernie fumble with response to BLM interruptions at his rallies, part of me was like, *Oh . . . maybe this is not the place for me.* I was uninterested in going to work somewhere where it seemed the boss did not get it, "it" being why young Black people felt the need to insert themselves in this conversation and proclaim that Black lives matter. But then they called me.

So about a week later, as I was running around doing Capitol Hill visits with some juvenile justice advocates, my phone rang. "The senator wants to meet with you today— are you available?" I told the aide I was only available until four p.m., and then I wouldn't be available until after seven. It was two thirty p.m. at this point. She asked if I were at all flexible on the hours. I said, "No, but I'd love to meet with him." She asked if she could call me back. We hung up. The phone rang again: "Can you come right now?"

I decided to go to the meeting because: one, you just don't tell a sitting United States senator no when he wants to talk to you; two, I thought it would be an opportunity to express my thoughts to him; and three, I hadn't gotten any other callbacks (HA).

PIECE OF ADVICE

A WORD ON HOW YOU LOOK
AND WHO YOU ARE

A word of advice about appearance and so-called normalcy. I am all for personal expression and finding a way to let your unique character show through details in your appearance. We come from different backgrounds and cultures and heritages and have different senses of style as individuals. Decorum dictates that in certain environments and situations, we dress to certain standards. That's fine. That doesn't mean we need to dress like everyone else, or that we need to change how we look in order to fit people's expectations. Once when I was on CNN a viewer wrote me a comment that my nails weren't "appropriate when talking about politics" on television. To that I say, there are lots of people telling us what we can't do and very few people encouraging us and telling us what we can do.

I think people—especially young people in industries where oftentimes there are not a lot of folks that look like them—should strive to blaze trails and do the things that haven't been done before. It wasn't normal for a really long time for women to wear pants in the workplace until somebody started wearing pants. And now nobody thinks twice about a pantsuit. But somebody had to be the one to put on the pantsuit. Make that person you.

At my first internship in DC, they told me that

folks only wear three things in this city: blue, black, and gray. I thought, Oh my God! I was about to wear a color-block jumpsuit tomorrow! *But you know what? I went to work in my color-block jumpsuit because that's who I am. I like making it my personal mission to show up as my authentic self every single day—because my authentic self is absolutely appropriate. I have the right to be who I am, whatever the circumstances.*

If I waited on someone to pick me, I'd be waiting for a really long time, and I probably wouldn't be talking to you in this book. I'm fully aware that when I show up curvy, with a low cut, a bold lip, an oversized bow, amazing nails, and a chilling analysis . . . people don't know how to take it. Because I am not supposed to be able to give you solid political commentary with a bedazzled nail, right?

Blaze a trail. Break the mold. Be who you are.

But, while I mean it when I say you should always be yourself, I also mean you should be your best-put-together self when the occasion calls. Keep some business wear in the trunk of your car, and at your office if you have one. You never know who might show up, or where you

might get invited to when you are out running
errands in your sweatpants. A little effort goes
a long way, whatever effort that may be.

I ran out of a congressional building to my car, grabbed a blazer and shoes out of my trunk, and booked it to Senator Sanders's office. When I arrived, Bernie came out and said, "Come on in!" I thought to myself, *This is not a normal workday.* And then I thought, *Why should it not be?* Why should it not be "normal" for a sitting senator and presidential candidate to talk to an informed and ambitious twenty-five-year-old Black woman? The fact that I even asked myself that question, though, is interesting. I questioned why things were the way they were, and decided the answer was that it did not have to be that way. It was kind of surreal. In the moment, I didn't grasp the significance, but I definitely thought, *I have something to say.* And I am glad I went in and I said it.

We had only said a few words to each other when we led right into the start of a joke that we would go on to make hundreds of times: yep, we have the same last name. "Maybe we're related," he said, and I was like, "Well, my dad's from Mississippi, so I dunno . . ."

From that oh-so-awkward start, the dialogue went something like this.

```
SENATOR:  I  didn't  know  there
were  so  many . . .
ME:  Black  people  in  Nebraska?
SENATOR:  I  was  gonna  say  Demo-
crats.
```

Ha ha, ha ha. More small talk; more getting-to-know-you chatty conversation. He asks me about school, about my current work, and then we get down to business. Anything you might have thought I would ask, I asked and the senator of course had thoughtful responses. We discussed Netroots, his reaction to the protestors, and overall strategy. Then we got into an argument. As the senator promptly let me know, we had "a fundamental disagreement" about economic policy. I suggested there was valid criticism out there about his policy, and he obviously did not agree. He then gave me his spiel about inequality and concentration of wealth and how politics is controlled by Wall Street.

Here's the thing: I don't necessarily disagree with the spiel—but he was missing a bigger issue. I started off trying to say something about how racial inequality in this country is not a subset of some other set of issues. But instead of fighting, I decided to backtrack and tell the senator a story that I'll share with you now.

I was on my way to the library one night in my car while I was in college. My parents lived in Omaha, near the university, and I was driving back from their house—it was around ten p.m. on a weekday. My taillight was out; I got pulled over. The officer ran my license.

"Ma'am, did you know you have a warrant out for your arrest?"

A warrant? That's just not possible. I've never been in trouble with the police before, ever. For what?! It turns out, he told me, I had a, uh, small number of parking tickets, let's say. At this point it had escalated to a bench warrant—which means I had to come in to deal with it. I asked, "Can I pay the tickets right now?"

Officer was like, "No, ma'am, that's not how it works— I'm gonna have to take you to jail." *Oh my God. I cannot believe this is happening.*

I got out of my car; he handcuffed me. I started crying as I got into the back of the police vehicle. Then I realized I couldn't wipe my nose because my hands were cuffed, so the tears stopped. There was another officer in the car too. I told them I was a student at Creighton. The other officer was like, "Oh, my wife went to Creighton"—I was thinking they'd let me go. No dice.

At this point in my story, I told the senator: I dunno if you've ever been to jail, but when you go, only one car is allowed in the parking stall at a time, because they don't want folks mingling when you get out. So we were waiting for a few minutes, and then one of the officers came around to open my door, but he told me not to move. I saw him bend down like he was picking something up off the ground. Then he told me I could get out (easier said than done with your hands cuffed) and he took me up to stand at the door to wait to be buzzed in.

Then, as this was happening, one of the officers said, "Oh, we found your weed."

I wasn't paying attention, because I didn't smoke, and so I didn't think they were speaking to me. So I didn't respond. "You hear us? We found your weed." My thoughts were racing, wondering what the hell they could be talking about. I didn't smoke. I hadn't been driving around with anyone who did. They couldn't possibly have found weed in my car, so why would they say such a thing? My mind switched into overdrive, trying to flip through all the possibilities of how I could prove this was impossible. While freaking out on the inside, I kept completely quiet.

They took me to holding, where they removed my jewelry. I said I was an intern in the mayor's office and I worked closely with my city council member. I tried my best to keep my cool, but my voice was trembling. Because I knew I had not done anything, but this is how folks' lives and futures get derailed—this is how "they" get you. This kind of thing could not only completely throw my life off track at the moment, but also sabotage my future.

What followed was a twenty-minute ordeal where they tried to convince me that I needed to take ownership of this marijuana that wasn't mine. I increasingly realized they were trying to pin it on me. I said it wasn't my marijuana; I didn't smoke. After an extensive back-and-forth, the officers gave up on getting me to capitulate to owning the pot, but not before letting me know that actually the weed they found wasn't very good.

I promptly retorted they should tell that to the person that sold it to them because it was not my marijuana. At this point, I'd had enough of their mind games, and I felt my confidence start to flood back into my bloodstream. I was innocent, and there was no way I was going to let them say anything to the contrary. I mean, they ignored my comments because . . . they knew just as well as I did that this was a bunch of bull.

They took my fingerprints, a mug shot, put a bracelet on me with my picture on it. Then I was moved to a holding cell with other women, a cell that was the size of a small closet, and there were twenty or so women in there. It wasn't a socializing kind of place; people are reeeeal quiet when they're waiting in jail. Finally, I was told I could make a phone call. I called my dad, told him I was in jail, and I instructed him to please call Ben Gray, my city councilman, and alert Stacy Westbrook (the special assistant to the mayor who had helped me get a job), because the officers tried to get me to take ownership of marijuana that wasn't mine.

My dad and mom came down to the station immediately. Because I was there on account of a bench warrant,

I was told I could post bail, or I could sit in jail until the next day, i.e., midnight. By the time my parents got there, it was eleven fifteen, so I just waited forty-five minutes. As I was telling Bernie this story, he was flipping out. "What?! How? Where did this happen?!"

I was like, "Omaha, NEBRASKA!!!"

This was my own experience, but it happens all over the country. It's happening right now. The only difference between Sandra Bland and me is that I had access and opportunity that helped me to get out of that awful situation.

I concluded to the senator, that was why I thought he should talk about race and justice issues being parallel to and intersectional with the issues in the economy. Because while the economic situation needs to change, nothing happens in a vacuum. No one cared what school I went to, that I worked at the mayor's office, what my parents did when I got arrested. That day the officers pulled me over and attempted to pin marijuana on me, all they saw was a Black girl driving through the north side of town, and that's all that mattered. It didn't matter what kind of job Sandra Bland had, the police decided she "talked too much." If we look at improving lives only through the lens of the economy, we're leaving out race and the implicit bias that goes along with it, which is very real.

Bernie had kept quiet while I had recounted this story, but his facial expressions said it all. So after I finished, I was pretty sure that Bernie and I had reconciled, but I waited for him to speak. The rest of our conversation went something like this:

```
SENATOR: I think I like you.
ME: I think I like you too.
SENATOR: I think I want you to
work here.
ME: I think I want to work here
too.
```

Then Senator Sanders asked me something none of the other twenty-nine interviewers ever asked me.

```
SENATOR: Do you have an idea of
what you want to do?
ME: Yes. I want to be your na-
tional press secretary. I want to
do cable television, and I want to
have a hand in the messaging strat-
egy just like we discussed here.
SENATOR: Have you ever done ca-
ble television before?
ME: No, sir, but I think I'd be
very good at it.
SENATOR: [Laughs.] Someone's go-
ing to call you. We'll be talking
to you soon.
```

Now, did I think that they were going to make me national press secretary? Not necessarily, but I figured I would go big then negotiate from there if I had to.

So, please, folks, always have an answer to the question "What do you want?": Out of your life. Or for dinner. You don't want to be hemming and hawing as the waitress gets agitated. You don't want to be sitting there figuring out your order when opportunity comes knocking. So set the bar high. The point is, I could have gone to work at Deloitte twenty-six interviews prior and been making a lot of money, but I didn't want that—I needed to stay on the path. I moved to DC because I wanted to work in politics—so if I wasn't working in politics, then what was the point? Always be ready with an answer to that question so when someone asks it, and that someone is the right person to give you the opportunity, you look prepared.

My meeting with Bernie was on a Thursday; that Sunday he was on *Meet the Press*. On Monday, I watched clips and saw he'd used the messaging I'd suggested: that economics and race are parallel issues that have to be addressed simultaneously! I was ecstatic. I called my mom to tell her and she was like, "That's great! Do you have a job?" Um. Good question, Madre!

The next day, Jeff Weaver called me back. He started talking about a phone and a laptop. Then I asked, "Jeff, what's my title?" and he said, as if it was obvious: "National press secretary." Ask for what you want, folks.

If we're always thinking about our lives and personal and professional goals through the lens of what has been normal up until that point, we maintain the status quo. If we think about our engagement with issues and the ways to effect change based on what has been done before, we are maintaining the status quo. We need to think about what's POSSIBLE, not normal. The idea of normal is just what we're used to. We shouldn't think about change or how we want to live our lives based off the idea of "being normal" or conforming to what has always been.

So, after getting off the phone with Jeff and being on a total high, I started to come down a bit. I was up on the issues, in general. I've always been a high-information voter, and I had been involved in issue-based advocacy for quite some time. But I wasn't sure exactly what I was getting myself into at that stage, at that level. Believe it or not, I am naturally a very risk-averse person—that's why I talk so much about taking risks. I need daily pep talks, from myself to myself. I have a lot of number one fears, including getting run over by a train in my car. (I used to work for the railroad—one of my 1,001 internships was at Union Pacific! They are based in Omaha—remember I told you the UP execs would be at church with the rest of us?) My most relevant fear in this instance is making the wrong decision, one that will lead me down a path I'm not supposed to be on, missing out on what I'm really meant to be doing. That career FOMO makes me hesitate. It's not the FOMO we feel when we think everyone is at some amazing party that we weren't invited to. It's the feeling that there was some other door open to me at one point that I chose not to walk through, one that would have led me down a different and perhaps better path. I work to overcome that particular type of FOMO so that when opportunities come, I can be confident enough to take them. Making decisions is a luxury, I remind myself. And I'm so lucky to have so many doors to choose from.

So, thinking about all of this, after a hot second of being so excited about taking a job with Bernie, all of a sudden I had a bit of a crash. I left Bernie's office after my first job interview and called a couple of people I considered mentors. In fact, some people I started calling and talking to, people I'd worked for or with in the past, said that there was a risk I was ruining my career, that I'd never get another job. People I really respect were telling me this! They said that I'd be branded a LEFTIST and it would be the worst thing ever! I remember thinking, *Wow, maybe I'm making the wrong decision.* A few of them were like, "AH! This could be the worst idea. Just wait. We can get you a job somewhere else, just wait." I had been on thirty freaking interviews. Wait for who? For what?

One of the people I called to talk things through was Shawna Francis Watley—a family friend from Omaha who lives in DC now and works for Holland & Knight, a major international law firm. Our families are super close; she's like an auntie to me. I told her about the job, and

I said I'd told Bernie I wanted to take it, but that all of a sudden, I was having doubts. She asked, "Is anybody else offering you a national press secretary position?" I was like, "No one's offering me anything!" Now, Shawna was Team Hillary. "He ain't gonna make it past February, Symone! But I think it'll be a really great experience. No one will be able to take it from you. If you like him and you're comfortable with the conversation you had with him, do it!" When opportunity knocks, just remember: Do all the people giving you advice have experience in what you're about to do? Had anyone I talked to ever been a national press secretary? No! Is it normal for them? No! Does that mean it's wrong for you or for me to do it? No!

In your career and in your life, look for guiding lights: people who open up a new path toward what normal can be. For me, one of those people has always Donna Brazile. I admired Donna from afar long before I met her. I used to watch her on TV, and she was so inspiring: the first Black woman to run a presidential campaign, someone who spent thirteen years as a commentator on CNN— she's just amazing. I met her early on during my time with Bernie's campaign, on the trail in 2016. I had only recently started doing TV, and we were in New Hampshire. We had set up a remote CNN location; I was back there getting my makeup done, and in walked Donna Brazile. I was like, *Oh. My. GOD.* I was trying to subtly ask the makeup artist to hurry up so I could go say hi.

My hero had just walked in! I tried to calm my fangirl self down, and then I got ready to say hello. She was on the phone, so she waved. Okay. So I went off and did my television hit, but I was still thinking about Donna, so afterward I went back to the staging area and she was still there. I went over to her, introduced myself. She said, "Oh, Symone. I know who you are." *Oh my God, DB knows who I am!* I tried not to shriek. As calmly as I could, I asked her, "Can I sit with you until it's time for your hit?" She said, "Sure." And then she started asking *me* all kinds of questions: how the campaign was going, how folks were treating me, my opinions on politics. Then she introduced me to everyone there—including Hilary Rosen, whom I affectionately like to refer to as one of my fairy godmothers. They were talking to me about TV and politics, and I felt like I just fell out of some other dimension into a childhood fantasy. Donna said, "Take my number. If you need anything, you let me know."

Of course, in this business, you always end up needing something. And I felt fortunate to have someone with the experience like Donna to bounce ideas off of, to ask her opinion, to help me figure out my way. I remember calling her later in 2016 to complain. I guess I expected a pat on the back or a word of sympathy or whatever, but I'll never forget what she said. "Symone, if you can't handle a little sexism and ageism at this level, perhaps this isn't the job for you." *Isn't the job for me? I worked hard to get here! This level?*

I'm not done, I thought. But I kept quiet, thank God. And I sat with her statement and thought about it for a while before I figured out what she was saying. Basically: ageism, sexism, racism—none of these things are going to go away tomorrow. You have to call things out when you see them; we have to work to combat these "isms," but . . . we also have to work through them. The world isn't going to change overnight. We have to move through it in the way it is now, doing the best we can while also agitating for change.

While you are trying to challenge the idea of *normal*, you have to wake up every day, toughen up, and get the job done. Her tough-love statement still echoes in my head whenever someone ruffles me. And I also reflect on our first meeting frequently. Sometimes you meet your sheroes, people you have looked up to, and it's underwhelming or disappointing. That was not my experience with Donna Brazile at all. I remember how I felt when she was just so open and inviting and warm and willing to talk to me. I try to be that way with people I meet on the trail, especially young folks. I might be exhausted or starving or stressed out, but I take the pictures, answer the questions, shake people's hands. I talk to every single person who wants to talk with me. Because my interaction with Donna literally changed my life and made me believe that a new idea of "normal" truly was possible for me, and I want to be the Donna to all the young Symones out there too.

Why are people so attached to the idea of normal, anyway? I suppose because it represents being comfortable. It gives us a sense of security. If we're always living our lives in terms of what's possible rather than what's comfortable, it's unsettling—there's no blueprint. People are scared of change. Normalcy is comforting, gives us a baseline for what to aspire to and what to yearn for, as long as it's something we recognize. It would be normal for me to go to school, graduate, find a job, find a partner, get married, settle into a career, probably have kids. For a lot of people, it's not normal to live off the grid on a homestead farm, or for a Black girl to act as a spokesperson for a candidate for president. But normal is just context. Someone else's normal is different from yours.

Fast-forward: all those people who told me not to take the job were wrong.

Think about whose definition of *normal* we've been living in for most of history. Straight, white men have been defining the terms according to their comfort, without concern for inclusion of anyone else. But by subscribing to not only their idea of normalcy, but the idea of normalcy as good, we're basically saying patriarchy and white supremacy are okay! We allow other people and the system at large to continue having power over us if we seek too much corroboration and validation from them, if we look to other people for approval of decisions.

Another thing we need to do: Stop asking for permission.

From anyone. Because the surprising thing is that sometimes it's the people close to you, the ones who you trust the most, who can really hold you back or kill your dreams. They may even think they are helping you when they tell you to be realistic, or reevaluate your capacity. Sometimes they are stuck in a previous understanding of you: they may have known you since age twelve or twenty, and they are stuck remembering a version of you that no longer exists. Or they simply think they have license to tell you how you should live your life, or imagine your future.

But to them, and to you, I say this. Every single time the needle has moved in American politics, the people who did the pushing were those considered outside the "norm." We would still be attending segregated schools if young people of color didn't get engaged and involved and push back against what was considered "normal." Women still wouldn't have the right to vote if people like suffragettes Alice Paul and Lucy Burns hadn't endured police beatings and jail time to make it so. We would not have marriage equality. We would not be having a national conversation about racism and its correlation to police brutality. Folks would not be working so hard to fix our criminal justice system.

If you actually want to do something in this world, you have to get engaged and involved. You have to stand up and speak out. For some people, that's running for office. For some people, that's being an outside agitator, like BLM leaders, for instance. For other people, it's being an attorney that represents people who need legal aid but can't afford it, or acting from the inside to write change-making policy. Whatever it is, one cannot afford to sit on the sidelines when one wants the game to change.

It wasn't "normal" for Bernie Sanders to hire me, a young Black woman, as his national press secretary when he campaigned for president. It wasn't "normal" in 2016 for candidates to willingly discuss universal health care, gun safety, immigration, abortion, and a whole host of other topics that we now consider absolutely fair game in questioning the credibility and fitness of our next president. Because we the people of the Democratic base have *redefined* what we want to think of as normal.

Democrats are more liberal than they were fifteen or even five years ago. It's not just that all of the candidates out there running for the Democratic nomination are more liberal; it's the constituents themselves. We are changing the very definition of *normal*: 46 percent of Democrats and Democratic-leaning voters now identify themselves as liberal—that figure was 28 percent ten years ago. Compared to twenty-five years ago, when 32 percent of Democrats said that immigrants strengthen our country, now 84 percent do. In the past ten years, the percentage of

Democrats who say that the government needs to do more to fight racism grew from 57 to 81 (Pew Research Center, US Politics and Policy Study 2018). We are redefining the boundary lines of our political parties. We are redefining what it means to be "normal."

4
CALLING ALL RADICAL REVOLUTIONARIES

(AND THE REST OF US TOO)

For us to better understand who "we" are, claim the power that we can, and redefine the meaning of *normal*, we need people who are willing to push the boundaries, be out in front of the crowd on the issues, put their lives on the line for the causes they believe in. It's these radical revolutionaries that lead the way in making a better life for the rest of us—we the people demanding change from outside the apparatus, and those with access pushing for change from within.

There are many different types of people playing the role of radical revolutionary; I see them in three broad categories: activist, academic, and practitioner. Like I said before, I'm not an activist; I just play one on TV. Of course I'm being a little facetious, but I'm also being honest. I know people who risk everything in support of a movement, who put their safety and well-being and career aspirations aside because they believe in a cause. As a political operative, I think of myself as a "practitioner" type of radical revolutionary. We need people out there pushing for change, and we also need people who can broker the exchange of ideas between the activists and the people currently in power. We need people radically committed to social justice, and practitioners who can put on a suit and stand in front of a jury and a judge and argue the finer points of the law effectively. We need voters, especially young people, willing to engage in the issues and rally others behind the candidates that promise revolutionary change—and then who are willing to hold these people accountable once they take office.

Demanding change requires time, commitment, and millions of people, filling different roles, in partnership.

The millennial generation is one of the most radical, revolutionary factions in our country today. Since we were children, we've been told over and over, "You can do anything you put your mind to." So let's do it. Let's demand progressive, programmatic reform. Let's push the Democratic Party to create new ideas even if they seem radical or overly idealistic. Let's create a new version of America.

It's far from an impossible task. After all, most of the ideas that the "powers that be" will try to convince you are "radical," or impossible, are no less valid than many of the questionable capitalist ideas the government has pushed and promoted over the past three decades (ahem: tax cuts for the wealthy, government-sanctioned student loan debt, questionable immigration policies, etc.). So there is absolutely no reason, in one of the richest, most diverse, and best educated countries in the world, why we can't have: universal health care, affordable college education, a justice system that actually works, young people under thirty-five IN CHARGE, TV panels that feature only people of color.

Radical is what some people use to describe something that we think is unattainable because it hasn't been achieved before. The question isn't what has happened in the past, but rather what is possible for the future? Framed that way, everything named up above is possible. But just because it's possible doesn't mean it's going to feel great getting there. There's going to be heartache, struggle, and loss.

Thankfully, there are plenty of examples from history that we can call upon to bolster our courage and commitment. We can also look to the past for evidence that although revolutionary change usually requires incremental steps, it doesn't have to move at a glacial pace. (Of course, "glacial pace" doesn't mean much anymore in our era of climate change; our glaciers are setting new records for their rate of disappearance. A critical and hugely urgent issue that requires radical revolutionary action NOW.)

For instance, consider that before the Civil Rights Act of 1964, there was a Civil Rights Act of 1957, and another in 1960: the first act established the United States Commission on Civil Rights and the United States Department of Justice's Civil Rights Division, the second created federal inspection of local voter registration polls. Neither did much that affected Black people's daily lived experiences, and they were neither radical nor sweeping by any means. It was not until four years later, after riots, lives lost, boycotts, sit-ins, and inspirational rhetoric that moved millions that we got the historic legislation of 1964 that codified the rights of Black people and minorities and outlawed discrimination.

There are several key traits of radical revolutionaries, whether you are talking about activists, academics, or practitioners. The first is that you have to be willing to buck the status quo and take a risk. The second, mentioned above, is that you have to get comfortable with being uncomfortable. And the third is that you must be willing to take on your allies as well as your adversaries. To illustrate these characteristics, I want to tell you about several people, different types of radical revolutionaries in their own times and contexts. Because that's another thing: context matters. The reality is that what's radical in Nebraska might not be so radical in Washington. What was radical in 1819 or 1919 or 1969 is not the same as today. For those reasons, I also want to talk about people who are pushing against the status quo in smaller or quieter but important ways, some of them working from inside the apparatus for change, complementing the work of those radical activists hammering away from the outside. Because everyone has a role to play. We need everyone in this fight.

One man who was both an academic and an activist, and who changed the way we think about the contributions of Black people in this country, was Dr. Carter G. Woodson. Woodson was the son of former slaves, born in 1875. He began his life working in the coal mines of West Virginia. He was the second Black man to earn a PhD from Harvard (after W. E. B. Du Bois). And he is the reason that we recognize Black History Month.

BLACK HISTORY MONTH

Lemme pause for a minute and say the fact that Black History Month falls in February is a major affront to some people. "It's the Man trying to get us down, relegating Black History Month to the shortest month of the year." I've heard people say this more than once. No, y'all. It's the fact that Dr. Woodson, who launched the idea of Negro History Week in the 1920s, decided that what was then a weeklong celebration of Black contributions to American history should take place during the week that contained the birthdays of both Abraham Lincoln, February twelfth, and Frederick Douglass, February fourteenth. So it didn't have anything to do with February being a short (or cold or miserable) month.

As an academic, Dr. Carter G. Woodson championed African American studies as a discipline worthy of research. Not only that, he paved the way for other disciplines like women's studies and LGBTQ studies by making the case that groups of disenfranchised people should have their contributions to history taken seriously. Dr. Woodson pioneered the idea that Black history should be preserved and celebrated even when his contemporaries said that Black history was just a piece of broader American history, that it didn't need any special attention or recognition. Dr. Woodson disagreed. He believed "Those who have no record of what their forebears have accomplished lose the inspiration which comes from the teaching of biography and history." And he believed that the distinct contributions of Black Americans were worthy of study and remembrance. He began the Association for the Study of Negro Life and History in 1915, and the academic *Journal of Negro History* in 1916. He became affiliated with the NAACP (founded in 1909) but grew frustrated by what he saw as a lack of commitment to revolutionary change to improve the lives of Black people. As Woodson put it, "I am a radical. I am ready to act, if I can find brave men to help me." He didn't wait around for people to get on board with his ideas. He went out and began speaking and teaching and agitating by himself.

By 1929, Negro History Week was being celebrated across the country. In 1970, an intergenerational group of students and faculty launched a monthlong recognition of Black History Month at Kent State University. Six years later, though Woodson had long since passed away by this point, President Ford announced as part of the US bicentennial that February would officially be designated as Black History Month. Dr. Woodson went from the son of slaves to a Harvard PhD who forever ensured the recognition of Black Americans' contributions to history.

Our era has old and new challenges and needs its own change makers. Young people have always been drivers of change—that's because we're not jaded; we haven't seen and done it all before. We come to the situation and see it for what it is. We aren't afraid to fail. Back in the day, someone had to say, "I don't think it's right that we have to sit at the back of the bus." Today we (still) have to say, "I don't think it's right that we have unequal educational opportunities in this country." The lesson is that it's important to say "this is isn't right" as a first step.

Though we bring a fresh perspective and new ideas, some of the same struggles that Dr. Woodson encountered continue to persist today. We need our own radical revolutionaries today to question and fight against our country's racist policies and assumptions, people like Ibram X. Kendi. Kendi is a millennial Black man at the vanguard of the academic study of racist policies in America. But he didn't start out as an academic or an activist. Kendi wanted to grow up to play in the NBA. He never imagined he'd become a member of a different, more exclusive NBA—those who have won the National Book Award, one of the world's most prestigious literary prizes. (The number of Black people who have won the National Book Award: twelve, starting with Ralph Ellison, who won for *Invisible Man*.) Kendi's award-winning book, *Stamped from the Beginning*, explodes the idea "that ignorance and hate lead to racist ideas, [which] lead to racist policies." Kendi says, "If the fundamental problem is ignorance and hate, then your solutions are going to be focused on education, and love and persuasion."

But, of course, *Stamped from the Beginning* shows that "the actual foundation of racism is not ignorance and hate, but self-interest, particularly economic and political and cultural." His latest book, *How to Be an Antiracist*, showcases the sort of fundamental reimagining that we still need to undertake as a nation when it comes to combating racism. As Kendi puts it, "No one becomes 'not racist,' despite a tendency by Americans to identify themselves that way. We can only strive to be 'antiracist' on a daily basis, to continually rededicate ourselves to the lifelong task of overcoming our country's racist heritage." As part of his mission to help do so, Kendi founded the Antiracist Research and Policy Center at American University. There Kendi inspires students to take up the fight as change makers, whether they be activists, academics, or practitioners, with the knowledge that to create real and lasting change in combating racism, our focus should be on changing policy instead of people.

As for me, I don't want to overstate my own contribution in pushing against the status quo, but I do believe I'm making an impact as a practitioner of radical, revolutionary change. The fact that a young, bald, Black woman was a regular commentator on cable news in the first place is kind of revolutionary.

It wasn't the easiest entrée into television, or politics. When I was out on the campaign trail in 2016 as Senator Sanders's national press secretary, there were many times when I would travel with the campaign and would arrive places for an event or rally, and I couldn't even get in. This happened for the first couple months on the campaign trail. I would go to the staff entrance. They would say "This is for staff," I would say I am staff, they would say "This is for campaign staff," I would say I am campaign staff. They would tell me I had to go around to the front, I would refuse, I would have to call someone and have them validate who I was, and I would often be late. This happened all the time. Not every single place, but consistently. So much so that on one Friday before a Saturday event, I called our advance team, the people who go ahead on the trail and make sure that everything, like logistics and lighting and security and lodging, is set up, and said, this is when I'm arriving, I'm driving this kind of car, can you please tell security working the event that I'm coming, can you also add that I'm bald and I'm Black. And they laughed, and I said, you tell them that I'm coming, you tell them what kind of car I'm driving, I can't take being late tomorrow. So please tell them.

I showed up Saturday. I pulled up in my Chevy Cruze, went to the first checkpoint, and security detail gave me so much trouble. Finally, I said, "Did the advance team not tell you I was coming? Did they tell you I was bald and Black?" Second checkpoint, I rolled down my window.

The guy said, "They told me you were coming." Third checkpoint was just a parking spot with my name with a little sign. I pulled up, and these two men came running up to my car, telling me I gotta get out of here, the space isn't for me—*move, now!* I sat in my car and I just started crying. Because I just wanted to go to work. I called our security folks, I called our campaign staff, and they came down and met me and talked to the assholes and then took me into a holding area. I put myself together, knowing the senator and his wife were about fifteen minutes behind me. And I still had to go to work.

The senator and his wife showed up. I started explaining what it was we were going to do, what press we were going to talk to, and the senator's wife, Jane, interrupted me and said, "Symone, what's wrong?" I broke down and ugly cried, and I told them what had happened. Before Jane could say anything else, the senator said, "Well, why can't you get in?" And Jane said, "Well, racism, Bernie." *Yes, Jane*, I thought, *and perhaps a little ageism and sexism too.* And then the senator said something profound. He said, "If you can't get in, who else is being kept out of the building that we don't know about?" Part of being a radical revolutionary in this moment is thinking about who else is being kept out of the proverbial building. Is our work putting anyone at a disadvantage? Who else are we not thinking about? Who are the people not at the table? Who are the people on the menu?

As I mentioned before, some radical revolutionaries take on the role of activists, some become practitioners, some others work from inside of academia, fueling the creation of new ideas and their implementation on a granular level. We need people enacting risk taking on an ideological scale. Think about the last presidential race: people now talk openly and regularly about these ideas that were so radical five years ago—gay marriage, universal health care, even guaranteed minimum income. That's because people took risks to associate themselves with these ideas and to push hard for them. Part of being a radical revolutionary is figuring out how to shift the moment, how to introduce an idea in a way that will gain traction. Before we had gay marriage, we had civil unions. The system doesn't want to open itself up to change; it doesn't want to allow radical revolution to take root and gain momentum. We have to find entry points. We have to find a way to begin to blaze the trail, if no path already exists.

It doesn't have to take forever for a movement to come together—look at the Women's March, for instance. The main rally in Washington that took place on January 21, 2017, came together in mere months. By now you've probably heard that the idea started with a few Facebook posts that immediately popped up in the wake of Trump's election on November 8, 2016. That's seventy-four days, y'all. To gather millions of women to march all over the country. To knit a sea of pink pussy hats. Of course, the struggle around issues of equal pay, equal opportunity, and equal standing for women has a long, long, legacy. But the organization of the march came together quickly, galvanized by protest of one of the most openly and egregiously antifemale presidents in recent history. What could have been a proud moment of women's solidarity didn't really end up that way, though. The intersectionality of the march, among women of different races, faiths, gender identities, and ages, was not what it could have been—both on the day of, and in the aftermath. It was a starting point, though, and a wake-up call for many about how much we can achieve if we come together, how much attention we can demand.

We all can take action. If you're on the board of a company, stand up and say the unpopular thing that you know is right. You might say, "You know what? I'd suggest that we do something different this year. Instead of putting the money toward X as we always do, I have a better idea: to contribute toward a more worthy cause that will have more of an impact." Or, "Let's cancel the PTA luncheon this year and use the money to fund a project at an underfunded school in our district." In the realm of politics, people like to say that members of Congress should just walk out whenever something egregious happens. C'mon. We do not elect members of Congress to walk out; it's their duty to sit in there and figure it the eff out. If getting the president impeached is your thing, a radical concept would be: organizing folks to come onto the Hill for the next three to four months; helping support a letter-writing campaign; writing and publishing op-eds. All of us need to do whatever we need to do, in our roles and in our contexts, to make change happen. Protests have their time and place. So do fund-raisers, phone-a-thons, filibusters, and "teachable moments."

I had a remarkable opportunity to connect with young potential change makers when I taught undergraduates at Harvard as a fellow at the Institute of Politics at the Kennedy School. How I ended up there is kind of a funny story: I applied for the fellowship in spring 2017. I wasn't accepted. So, case closed, I figured, and I moved on. Out of the blue in October 2018, I got an email from Amy Howell, the new executive director of the IOP. It was a Thursday when I heard from her, and she asked me if I could come to an event for the bipartisan women's group on campus. She told me the students had been lobbying for me to come. The event was on a Tuesday. I was like, *Are you kidding me?* I knew this was Harvard and all, but I was a little bit busy.

I was at an event later that night, a gala for the group Knock Out Abuse, which works with victims of domestic abuse, I bumped into Monique Pressley. She was like, "Symone, are you crazy? You have to go." So I agreed to do the event at Harvard. It was a small group of twenty young women who showed up, and I gave my talk and then we had a great dialogue. I heard from Amy again a few days after the event. She said, "I'm so sorry we didn't have a chance to talk in person, but I was sitting in the back of the room quietly inspired—and do you want to come be an IOP fellow this winter?" I laughed and wrote back and told her about my rejection. "Never mind that," she said, and a few months later I was back at Harvard, in residency, teaching a ten-week class. The university worked out a flexible schedule for me so that I could be there for a few days a week and then back in DC to keep doing my other work on CNN and elsewhere.

Looking back now, I realize that when I contemplated turning down my initial invite to Harvard, I almost missed a life-changing opportunity. The fellowship pushed me to think of myself as a teacher and a writer, which I'd never really done before. It sounds clichéd, but it's true: in the end I learned just as much from the students as they learned from me. I also interacted with a couple of other residential and visiting fellows to whom I probably never would have spoken otherwise, like Ed Gillespie, longtime GOP operative and a former Republican National Committee chairman who narrowly lost the race for governor of Virginia in 2017—and my new best friend. During our first week of orientation at the IOP, Ed and I were seated near each other at dinner. After a few glasses of wine and small talk, and in true Symone D. Sanders fashion, I decided to ask the burning questions I had about his gubernatorial bid. Ed definitely had answers and that was the beginning of our friendship. The IOP was a great reminder that conversations change things—people, circumstances, and even our political discourse.

During my time at Harvard, I invited a couple guest speakers to my class, young people who are standing up and making the statement "This isn't right," and doing something about it. I wanted my students to see examples of people involved in actively agitating for policy change, rather than only studying or talking about it. One of them was Samuel Sinyangwe. Here's the one-sentence version of Sam's early life: he has a Tanzanian dad and a Jewish mom, grew up in Florida, graduated from Stanford, and started working for a nonprofit in Oakland shortly after graduation. Then George Zimmerman shot and killed Trayvon Martin, an unarmed Black seventeen-year-old, in the neighborhood where Sam used to go to soccer practice. Sam's life changed that day. He immediately felt the impact of what had happened. "I could have been Trayvon. That's why it hit me so personally, and that's why I realized that I needed to be doing something [about the problem]." He started feeling distracted at work, but instead of wasting time on Instagram he got involved with the Black Lives Matter movement. But he wasn't content to stand on the sidelines of the movement; he wanted to use his knowledge and skills to make a real difference, to look for actionable policy solutions to the problems of violent police encounters with young Black people. So Sam cofounded Mapping Police Violence—the first comprehensive plotting of incidents across America. He then helped launch Campaign Zero, an organization focused on ending police violence, with fellow activists Brittany Packnett Cunningham and DeRay Mckesson. And so, at a very young age, Sam found himself inside the apparatus, speaking his radical message face-to-face with presidential candidates like Hillary Clinton and Bernie Sanders, offering advice about ways to address racist police brutality in America.

Another guest speaker in my Harvard class was Alencia Johnson, a young Black woman who served as director of public engagement for Elizabeth Warren's campaign, but at the time held the same job title at Planned Parenthood Federation of America. Planned Parenthood is an essential American institution now at the center of an epic battle for women's reproductive rights in this country, which are under assault in a manner not seen in fifty years. Alencia went to Planned Parenthood after working on Obama's reelection campaign in 2012 because she wanted to "shift public opinion and influence culture change among perceptions of reproductive rights, particularly among communities of color as well as young people." After joining PP, Alencia created her own department called Constituency Communications, in which she pushed Planned Parenthood to participate in the immigration fight, invest in Black women's leadership, and focus on women "left at the margins:

women of color, trans people, young people, low income folks and people in rural areas. [At the time] there was no campaign to speak to them specifically." Alencia made it her mission to change that, and PP is now at the forefront of the fight to maintain and strengthen women's reproductive rights.

Stories of people like Sam and Alencia remind us that it's important to consider that factions in the Democratic Party—millennials of color, Black women, activists—overlap, but they contain different constituencies, different communities of people with different needs and goals and priorities. Yes, the factions of the Democratic Party power the apparatus, but they also shape and drive the conversation. For many factions, that is their principal aim: to move the conversation, not necessarily to win mayoral elections, gubernatorial races, or seats in the House and the Senate. The members of these factions and their leaders care about the future of the *issues* of police brutality, marginalization of Black women in the workplace, justice reform, reproductive rights, and much more, but they do not necessarily care about the future of the Democratic Party as a whole. If the Republican Party was suddenly willing to push their agendas, some factions might find themselves moving to the other side of the congressional aisle. For some, party affiliation matters less to them than their issues and who will support them.

Now, I don't think there's going to be a major defection

any time soon. But it is worth considering, and it's also worth recognizing that factions themselves can fall victim to the same predilections of the apparatus. While we are correct to critique the apparatus, we cannot forget to examine the factions too. A faction like some of the women's movement groups who have historically written checks they couldn't cash: some claim to support all women, but center around the perspectives of white women; some advocate for women's right to choose, but aren't making sure Black and Latino women have the choice to equitable treatment in the workplace. Before any intersection of coalitions can occur, those coalitions respectively must be honest in keeping to their goals and delivering on what they say they are going to do. A collective mission cannot be achieved when everyone is operating with a to-each-their-own kind of attitude.

So how can the factions on the left best intersect? Where do we—millennials of color, Black women, progressives—go from here? First off, it's good to recognize we have made strides in shifting the status quo in the apparatus. For example, Tom Perez, the chair of the DNC, is the first Latino chair in its history. But what's most important is not that we have a colorful apparatus that functions the same way as it always has. We need a colorful apparatus that reflects the wants and needs of the colorful factions.

We also need more substantive color in the Democratic

Party—Black and brown mayors, governors, senators, and congresspeople not asking for but demanding change. Key leaders in factions of the Democratic Party need to look outside their straight line of vision to the others in their periphery working hard to achieve their own worthy aims. Perhaps we, as members of seemingly separate and independent factions, haven't yet tried hard enough.

That said, in further proof of progress, we now have some young radical revolutionaries sitting in some of the highest offices in the land, people like Alexandria Ocasio-Cortez, Lauren Underwood, Ayanna Pressley, and Sharice Davids. When you are an activist and you enter into education, politics, business, or other realms, sometimes you have to rethink your own activism and radicalism. What used to be a demand becomes a conversation, a collaboration, even, with people who are of a different mind-set than you—AOC now has a job to legislate, make deals, get things done. She's no longer just sitting outside protesting; that worked before, but her tactics have to shift now that her position has shifted. She's inside the apparatus. She has more access to real power. To yield that power to its greatest effect, she has to know how to work the apparatus from the inside out. We're all waiting to see how it's going to shake out in terms of her ability to create measurable change over the long run, but I admire what she's doing in the meantime.

For instance, she has been willing to call out Democrats

just as loudly as she does Republicans when she sees them falling down on the job, or just not living up to the expectations that people have of their leaders. AOC is out there, taking on her allies as well as her adversaries.

PIECE OF ADVICE

BE READY TO TAKE ON YOUR ALLIES AS WELL AS YOUR ADVERSARIES

Everyone reading this book, whether in your head or IRL, is willing to take on that person who is very obviously, and obnoxiously in many cases, ideologically different from you; you know you are waiting on them to say something so you can pounce, like waiting for the kid sister you're jealous of to screw up. It's easy to go to war when you have an enemy. But far too many of us are not willing to take on our allies, accomplices, friends, sorority sisters, fraternity brothers, when we see them acting in a way that's not in keeping with our values or beliefs. We're scared to upset the circle of people around us, to cause trouble in our own lives. But that's where real change and conversation happen.

Dr. King took on his allies when he stood up and questioned the same senators that helped him pass the Civil Rights Act and the Voting Act—when he went to them talking about fair housing and poverty, and these folks could not be bothered. The only reason we have the Fair Housing Act today is that in the aftermath of Dr. King's assassination, Congress rushed to pass the act to pay homage to him. Because when he asked for it, they told him no, he was crazy.

In a 1967 TV interview, MLK said pointedly that he realized a lot of the folks on the front lines with him in the lead-up to the Civil Rights Act weren't marching because they cared about racial activism. These were people who were responding to the extremeness of the treatment of Black people in the South. They were responding to the images of the fire hoses and the dogs. They weren't responding to the underlying issue. Much like now. We hear and see a lot of responding to the extremeness of our current political climate—to the president, to the kids in the cages at the border, separated from their families—but for the most part are we really thinking deeply about the actual issues?

There are people who say about the Democratic Party, why are we eating our own? But just remember, Dr. King spoke out against the Vietnam War when it meant going against people who had supported him on other measures. We need to learn to speak up and speak out, sometimes against the people who have always been with us. Because guess what: truth and justice don't care if I know you, whether we are friendly, whether we have a history. Sometimes to pursue the greater good, you have to be blind to personal allegiances and do what the situation demands. That's what this is really about.

Everybody knows about the Dreamers—the young folks brought to this country as minors by parents who immigrated illegally. Everybody wants to talk about them, but nobody wants to talk about how *we* got here. Back when Obama was president, Congress, as usual, failed to act. The immigration activist community, the Dreamers, all these groups felt defeated. There was a segment of folks that said, "We are going to keep fighting." Some people said, "Don't take on Obama; just wait, he's going to do the right thing." These other folks didn't wait; they didn't listen. They backed the White House into a proverbial corner. They made it very uncomfortable and politically untenable for the White House to *not* do something on this issue. That's where DACA (Deferred Action for Childhood Arrivals—the policy that allows some individuals who arrived in this country as the children of undocumented immigrants to defer deportment and become eligible for work permits) came from—not because President Obama woke up and said, "I want to do something good today," but because he *had* to act (thanks in large part to Congress's inaction). It was demanded of him, by an ever-bigger, ever-louder group of people. The people fighting for the Dreamers were willing to take on their allies. It's a lesson for the rest of us. We need to get serious about what it means if we want to be on the side of truth and social justice.

When people claim to be radical revolutionaries in the spirit of X or Y, they claim to be doing that really important social justice work; they claim to be the next Malcolm, Coretta, or whoever else. But they aren't doing the hard, uncomfortable work of being unpopular. In the weeks after Dr. King's assassination, some opinion polls said that Dr. King had brought his assassination upon himself. You know, he was a very hated man at that particular moment. Even people who had once been with him, who had supported or followed him, had turned against him. This was partially because people were pissed off that Dr. King had started going on about all this other stuff instead of civil rights, which was what the proverbial *they* thought Dr. King was only supposed to be about. According to them, that is. When Dr. King started pushing hard on issues of poverty, he wasn't just talking about Black people. He was talking about poor white people. Poor Asian American people. Poor indigenous people. Dr. King was saying that no one can truly enjoy the fullness of the American dream if he or she is hampered economically. Eradicating the slums, solving fair housing. These were things that some people said did not concern Dr. King, but he disagreed. That's what being a radical revolutionary requires: if we want to be good leaders, we must be good community members. You can't do that without standing up, even to people who have supported you in the past.

For instance, it was a sad and difficult moment when on the first day of Black History Month in 2019, a story broke that the governor of Virginia had appeared in a picture in his 1984 medical school yearbook dressed in a costume and blackface or as someone dressed up as a Klansman. Fast-forward a week; then we found out that the Virginia attorney general acknowledged that he had worn blackface at a party while an undergrad. Then the next thing you found out, hours later, was that the lieutenant governor was accused of sexual assault. I know the lieutenant governor; I considered him a friend, I worked on the campaign to elect him. When the news broke that a second woman had come forward and accused him of raping her while in college, I was on CNN. The producer came on during a break and said we were going to take the news live. Oh Lord. I had heard allegations earlier in the week and honestly hoped I would get through this segment without the news breaking. I was unsuccessful.

Jake Tapper came back to the panel, and on the air he said, "Symone, I don't want to put you in an awkward position"—in my head I was thinking, *Well, it's about as awkward as it gets*—"but you know the lieutenant governor; what do you think?"

Now let me tell you, at this point it was three months after a moment in the Kavanaugh hearings where I felt it necessary to share my story of assault. One night in college, I'd had too much to drink and someone whose advances I had previously rebuffed on numerous occasions took advantage of the fact that I could not consent. The next morning he denied raping me, but that is exactly what he did. I sat at that little clear Plexiglas table on CNN, and I shared what had happened to me.

Now I was sitting at that same table, on that same program, being asked how I was going to react to these allegations against the lieutenant governor, who was also a friend. So I said, "Jake, I know the lieutenant governor as a colleague, a friend, a brother, but I must say, I have been disappointed with how he initially chose to handle the allegations—disparaging the women's character. It has been disappointing, but hearing this I think he has to resign. I also think it's unfortunate that it seems the only person in Virginia who may suffer the consequences of their actions will be the Black lieutenant governor. I think some other people made bad choices and they gotta resign too, the governor included." And Jake went, "Even the attorney general?" And I was like, "If you ever wore blackface, assaulted someone, etc., I do not think you can serve. I think service is a privilege; it is not a right." Then the segment ended.

I knew what was coming. That night and weekend I got a lot of phone calls and a lot of emails from people I know personally. Folks telling me, *You didn't have a Black man's back. Why would you throw him under the bus?* But like I told y'all, it's not truth and justice with an asterisk that says *unless you know them. We will be faced with real-life decisions on a regular basis about who it is we really want to be, and where we want to stand when it comes to our values and allegiances.

5

GET OUT OF LINE

Who doesn't remember being told to wait your turn as a kid? Who doesn't remember being admonished to "be nice"? With apologies to Ms. Goose, my kindergarten teacher, I'm now going to have to tell you that if we want real change in our country, if we really want to address racial inequality, climate change, the mess that is our health-care system, the eroding quality of our public schools, our country's opportunity gap, we have got to wake up and get out of line. We need to act with the urgency that these problems require, and with the attitude that we can and will find solutions. Waiting in line and being nice aren't real options anymore.

I often wonder why everyone except older white men

are constantly being told that they need to "wait their turn." We need to deprogram ourselves, get over the brain-washing we've endured by hearing this message over and over and over. Growing up, folks told me that if I put my head down and worked hard, my talent and contributions would be recognized. I have since come to realize that this is simply, unfortunately, not true. Sometimes you can be the best—by virtue of natural talent, grit, intelligence, or hard work—and the proverbial "they" still might not pick you. Why? Perhaps because they don't think you're palatable enough. Or experienced enough. Or a good "fit." I've certainly been told each of those things.

But whatever the reason for the no, don't let them keep you from what's yours. I wouldn't be where I am today, working as a senior advisor to a Democratic presidential candidate at twenty-nine years old, if I had waited for permission or stepped back to let others who seemingly knew better pass. The most inspiring change makers I know grabbed their seats at the head of the table without waiting for a place to clear, or hanging out hoping for "the right time" to squeeze in.

Here's another thing. And now I'm looking directly at the ladies. We don't HAVE to be nice. We should all be kind, men and women alike, but this concept of "nice" in the sense of being deferential or accommodating is patri-archal bull. Niceness is a concept that only ever applies to women. Rarely do we hear someone telling a man to be nice! Men who are aggressive are told they are determined, competitive. Women are told they are being bitches. Be aware that fading into the background and putting aside your opinions if they aren't popular won't get you rewarded; more often it will just leave you frustrated. Don't get it twisted—I hope people think I'm a kind person, and a good person, but nice? Nah. I don't really care if they think I'm nice.

I'm a young, Black woman in a male-dominated field who defies expectations and the standards of white beauty every day. I don't have time for nice (since it so often means please shut up and go away), and neither do you. And honestly, look around at who's being called "nasty" these days by a certain someone in the White House. I'm just about ready to wear that word like a badge of honor.

Do you think Shirley Chisholm stood around waiting in line for the apparatus to permit her entrance, as the first Black woman elected to Congress? Do you think she became the first Black person to seek the presidential nomination by a major party by being nice, in the deferential, go-with-the-flow sense? Oh hell no. She was the daughter of immigrants, a father who was a factory worker, and a mother who was a maid. She grew up to be an "Unbought and Unbossed" champion for women's rights and racial equality (the phrase was one of her congressional slogans, and the title of her memoir). She's the one who helped pave the way for people including Congresswomen Maxine Waters and Eleanor Holmes Norton, who was once the boss of a young congressional intern who's now my personal hero, the aforementioned Donna Brazile.

Donna Brazile wrote in the introduction to Chisholm's memoir that Chisholm "did not wait for permission and she did not seek the acceptance of those who came before her. She was her own boss." Congresswoman Chisholm knew full well that "women in this country must become revolutionaries" and "refuse to accept the old, the traditional roles and stereotypes." She was a true master of making a way forward though no one wanted to let her through, though no path existed, and she left this trail for others to follow.

And she didn't stop once she got to a place of power. When Chisholm was first elected to Congress in 1968, representing New York's twelfth congressional district, she was dismayed to be assigned to the House Agriculture Committee, which she felt had little connection to her work with her urban constituents. But did she sit back, bide her time, fall in line? No. She met with Bob Dole, then a Republican senator from Kansas, and they worked together on the food stamp program, which allowed poor Americans to buy food staples at subsidized prices. She went on to help with the inception of the Special Supplemental Nutrition Program for Women, Infants, and Children (WIC) to make sure that these vulnerable populations had access to important food supplements.

She knew how to bring her adversaries on board as well as her allies. For instance, she reached out to the infamously racist George Wallace, an outspoken advocate of segregationist policies, after he survived an assassination attempt where he was shot at point-blank range. She recalled their interaction when she visited him in the hospital: "He said to me, 'What are your people going to say?' I said: 'I know what they're going to say. But I wouldn't want what happened to you to happen to anyone.' He cried and cried and cried." And you know what? Chisholm called up Wallace in 1964 when she was working on a bill to ensure domestic workers had a right to a mandated minimum wage, and Wallace helped get votes from Southern congressmen, enough to get the legislation passed in the House. Chisholm noted, "He always spoke well of Shirley Chisholm in the South. Many of the Southerners did not want to make the vote. They came around."

Shirley Chisholm overcame enormous odds. She grew up in a country that abolished slavery a mere sixty-one years before she was born. In just about another twenty years from now, and certainly by 2045, new government census data shows the United States will be "majority minority"—in other words, people of color will be the majority in this country. Women already outnumber men in America. So what does it mean that women and people of color are approaching majority? What does it mean that we're entering into positions of influence and power in greater numbers than ever before? What will change look like? That depends on us—what we're demanding, what we're asking for. We're in the middle of a cultural shift, and we need to take advantage of that. We won't get as far as we can as fast as we can if we're worried about stepping around people to get where we need to go, or worried about offending them or displeasing them along the way.

But before you start pushing out ahead of everybody else, remember: You have to be prepared. Know your stuff. Because you are going to be scrutinized and called to task for every single thing you say and do, in a way that others (see: white cis men) are not. For me, being a young person (often the youngest) in the room means I always have to have numbers, details, facts—otherwise everyone says I don't know what I'm talking about. Remember the run-in I mentioned with Santorum about the poopy lettuce? That happens. A lot.

Sometimes it's the voice in your head that most loudly questions your authority or capabilities. After all, it can be hard at times to overcome a lifetime of conditioning that tells us that we need to wait in line and be accommodating. Even when we decide to step out and take risks, sometimes *we* are the ones who are holding ourselves back, with self-doubts or recriminations, with insecurities or fear of failure, with a lack of self-knowledge.

Another consideration when stepping out of the line that you're supposed to wait in is that you need to know where your own lines are internally. What are you willing to do, or not do, to achieve your goals? What in your life is worth sacrificing for a cause that you believe in, and what is not? How vocal are you willing to be about the change you want to see in the world, and what are you willing to do or not do to see it come to pass? One thing is for sure: people are always ready to throw shade. In order to not let it reach you, you need to have a strong light guiding you from within. Others may have illuminated a path for you to follow along, but your own inner light, this self-knowledge, will help make clear your boundaries, what you are willing to do or not do. For me, this light comes from my faith in God and from my family, especially my parents, who instilled strong values in me about community and service.

It took some reassessment of the state of my own self-knowledge in order to feel confident about taking the next step in my political career. In April of 2019, the official announcement came out that I had joined the Biden campaign as senior advisor. Pretty much immediately, I started appearing on TV representing the former vice president. One of the first things that happened, as I mentioned earlier on, was that I was ambushed about the 1994 Violent Crime Control and Law Enforcement Act, which passed while Bill Clinton was president and Biden was Senate judiciary chairman. The $30 billion package included an assault weapons ban, funding for drug courts, the Violence Against Women Act, but it also included funding for additional prisons and supported tougher sentences for those convicted of crimes.

Critics of Biden immediately pounced and said that the bill contributed to the crisis of mass incarceration in this country, and that it was directly responsible for the huge problems we have today in our prison and criminal justice system. For instance, nonviolent first-time drug offenders are serving decades of time in prison: 49 percent of Black men aged twenty-three or older have been arrested at some point in their lives, according to a study conducted by the Obama White House in 2016. Also, the US represents 21 percent of the global prison population despite only having 4 percent of the world's people, according to a National Research Council report produced by an interdisciplinary committee of researchers. In other words, not a good scene. But to say that this one bill directly led to our problems of mass incarceration is more than a little simplistic. Nevertheless, I wasn't quite expecting to answer attacks on Biden about his role in our country's prison culture on basically my first day on the job. But I had to, so I did. Live on CNN.

I don't think people understand sometimes that my role is as an operative, a political operative. When you are an operative or an aide—that is, a *good* aide, a good spokesperson for your candidate or your principal—rule number one is that you don't get out ahead of your candidate. You wait for them to vocalize their opinions and their responses, and then you back them up. And while I have feelings and thoughts, I'm not going to express those thoughts or opinions to millions of people on CNN, because I'm a consummate professional ☺. So instead of getting out in front of Biden on this issue of the crime bill and mass incarceration, I twisted myself into a hot, salty pretzel to not say anything that he hadn't already said.

It is my job to support my principal and make him come out looking as best as he can, no matter the circumstances or the accusations. That can be confusing to some people, but I rely on my strong sense of personal integrity to pull me through. Nevertheless, in a word, the interview was terrible.

From the outside looking in, I could see that it was set up to look as if the campaign had sent me out there to talk about this issue, when in fact the media ambushed me. This interview was conducted right before Biden's first official rally in Philadelphia. There was so much I was excited to say about Biden's campaign launch and all the things he stands for, all the ways he could help improve the state of our economy, our foreign policy, our environment, our domestic issues of inequality. Was I expecting the media to grill me about the ins and outs of a twenty-five-year-old bill? No. But there I was, doing my job. What was I going to do when something like this happened—take my mic off and walk away? Refuse to answer? Give a blank stare? No. This was what I'd signed up to do. And honestly, digging into a candidate's record is something we should expect and desire from our media.

Sometimes you have to take a deep breath and focus on the long game rather than getting caught up in the painful moment. Moments like that do make you stop and question what you are doing, and that's not necessarily a bad thing. You should evaluate where your lines are, what you are willing to do and say in pursuit of your larger goals. I need to know that I can sleep soundly when I take my eyelashes off at night, confident in the knowledge that what I am doing is right, that I am working for someone who could definitely make America a better place. I feel that way in my work today; I felt it on previous campaigns too. That said, I understand my role and my lane.

PIECE OF ADVICE

KNOW YOUR OWN BOUNDARY LINES

Though I encourage everyone to do what they can to jump the lines that society puts us in, I also feel you need to find the personal and professional lines that you want to stay within; that is, your own internal boundaries. Far too many people haven't thought enough about this concept, and it can lead to real problems: reputational damage, hurt feelings, severed relationships, getting fired, and so on. Look at someone like Sean Spicer, who I knew socially before he went to work for Trump. Once upon a time, before he was a punch line, Spicer was a really good communications professional. He had worked in the business forever. But he messed up big-time, because he didn't understand his personal or professional lines—he lost his inner compass, tossed it aside in favor of doing what his boss wanted him to—and that caused him to flat-out lie on multiple occasions. Part of being a communications professional is that you don't lie. You can spin, you can fudge, but you do not lie for your principal. And frankly, a good boss would never ask you to lie—and that holds true in any industry.

The moment someone asks you to lie, to cross your professional lines, you have to make a decision about whether that is something you are willing to do or not. Part of taking on challenges is understanding your boundaries, whether you are in a relationship, whether you are at work, whether you are doing activism in pursuit of social justice. If you don't know where your boundaries are, your limits, how you will react to personal affronts or unreasonable demands then how will you be able to define what is and is not acceptable to you? You won't have the words to respond when someone insults you or asks you to do something that seems questionable, or inquires about your motives or actions, because you don't know what is and isn't acceptable to you as an individual. When you know your own boundaries, then you can find the answers when you ask yourself: Am I willing to work this shift, answer this question, sacrifice this vacation, put up with this person's attitude, live with this uncertainty, take this pay cut, relocate for this job?

I've been a line jumper for most of my life. I was never content to wait around when I saw so much in the world that I wanted to do. And I knew early on that to do the kind of things I wanted, I needed to be in DC. The first time I visited DC was with Girls Incorporated of Omaha. When I was thirteen or fourteen years old, I took part in a program called She Votes through Girls Inc., and that's how I discovered my passion for politics. The program introduces girls to the political process: how and why we need to vote, about women serving in positions of power, about different elected officials and what they do. In my year, there was a cohort of about six of us who came to DC—this was when Hillary Clinton was a senator. We had an opportunity to visit the Hill, we got a personal audience with Senator Clinton, and we visited the Girls Inc. national offices.

I was in love. This was what I wanted to do, and DC was where I wanted to be. Five or six years later, while in college, I served on the board of the National Coalition for Juvenile Justice and had the chance to start to really get to know Washington. I started coming back and forth regularly from Omaha for board meetings, two or three times per year. Then the summer after my sophomore year, I interned in DC at the national public policy office of Girls Inc. It was a rich summer and a poor summer. Rich with experiences, poor in that I was just scraping by since it was an unpaid position. I'm so thankful to the family friends who let me stay at their place, even if it was out in the boonies, in a suburb called Bowie. Every morning I got up at six a.m., walked a mile from the gated community to the bus stop, got on the bus, took the bus to the Metro, sat on a thirty- to forty-minute Metro ride, and then walked from the Farragut North Metro station to the Girls Inc. office. After that summer, I went back to Omaha, but I knew when I finished school that I would make DC my home. This was where I needed to be to make an impact on the largest level. Plus the city had a vibrancy, an energy, a feeling of possibility about it that I had never sensed anywhere else.

In the fall of 2014, I'd been working on Chuck Hassebrook's campaign for governor of Nebraska. The day after he lost, I was like, *Nope. Got to go.* So that day, I got on a plane to DC and crashed at my friend Amber's place. Even though I was sleeping on a couch, I still knew that this was where I wanted to be. I stayed for a couple of weeks, starting to hunt for an apartment, and then went back at Thanksgiving to see my family and get my car. My dad was like, "Symone, you're just going to get in your car and drive to DC? Do you have a place to live when you get back there?" "Nope, but I'm looking on Craigslist," I told him.

My mother was very supportive of what I wanted to do, but my father was very skeptical of me uprooting myself. There was no stopping me, though; I packed my life into my car, got in with my friend Aja, and we drove off back to DC. By December, I had moved into my own apartment with a roommate I'd found on Craigslist. My life was about to begin, albeit in a third-floor walk-up five miles out of the city center.

My first month in DC was miserable. When I first went to work at Global Trade Watch, it was a steep learning curve. On my first day they were using acronyms that were totally meaningless to me: *NAFTA—okay, got it. CAFTA? TAFTA? WTF?* I thought. Trade issues were very new to me at the time; everything I was writing came back with red ink all over it. I would go to work early and come home very late, and oftentimes I would have more work to do once I got there. I didn't know anyone, I didn't like my roommate, it was cold, I didn't have any money, and my job was hard. In other words, I was in my early twenties in a big city.

It was tough, but the truth is when I left Nebraska, I was stepping out of line—I was getting out of my comfort zone in a big way. And I moved because I wasn't going to hit the political jackpot at home. I knew moving to DC was what I needed to do, to take a chance on my dreams. But it was hard. I missed my family. My job was tough. I wasn't doing what I'd wanted or expected to be doing. But I knew I had to make it work. And, of course, once I got a little bit comfortable in DC and in my job, once I started building a network, I started getting a little impatient, and I knew

I needed to get out of line again. So I started interviewing. And I went to interview after interview after interview (twenty-nine of them, remember?) before I landed the Bernie Sanders job. I was trying not to get discouraged. My mom was saying things like "You can always come home." Yes, but I didn't want to come home! I appreciated her support, but I knew if I just went back, I would feel like a failure. I had to exhaust every option first, because I was unwilling to go back to standing in line.

After the crazy season of seemingly endless interviews, I suddenly found myself, at twenty-six, as the national press secretary of a man running to be the Democratic nominee for president of the United States. When I first started working on the Bernie Sanders campaign, I was confident—and just wanted to do a good job. Contrary to the expectations of everyone who inquired, I was not nervous. Even though I was entering a new territory professionally, even though I was very young, I knew myself: what I could accomplish and what I was willing to do. I would never have been offered the job if I hadn't just stepped up and asked for it. In my initial conversations with Bernie, when he asked me what I wanted my role to be, I could have thought, *Well, I have many years ahead of me in my career and I'm relatively inexperienced, so I should just take X position while I wait to become Y.* Nope. I asked for Y. And I got it. As you know.

The campaign itself was a real start-up-type situation

at this point. A week after I got a verbal offer, I still had nothing official. I thought to myself, *Did I dream all of this up?* No timeline, no protocols, nothing. So I was still working at the trade organization when Jeff Weaver called me up on the last Thursday in July. He said, "We're so happy you work here, kid. How do you feel about coming out on the campaign trail in Seattle next weekend with the senator? Not in your capacity as press secretary quite yet, but in your role as a juvenile justice advocate?" He mentioned that the weekend would be the anniversary of the death of Michael Brown. *Hmm,* I thought. *This doesn't feel quite right. Why still not in my official role? Is this a test for whether they are going to officially hire me? But—am I going to say no to this opportunity?* I cut right to the point: Am I going to get paid? Jeff said no because I would not be acting in my official capacity as press secretary, but all my expenses would be covered. "I need you to write a speech," he told me, "because you'll intro the senator to the crowd. Oh, and what's the largest crowd you've ever done? We're thinking fifteen thousand people at this thing."

Oh. The biggest crowd I'd addressed to that point was when I introduced Bill Clinton in front of a crowd of three to four thousand people when I was sixteen at an event for Girls Inc. But I could do this. I knew I could do this! This was my moment, the one I'd been waiting for and working toward. If I nailed this speech, it could change my life. So I got to work. I wrote my speech. It began by talking about the anniversary of Michael Brown's death (which was the next day). I went on to name many others who had been victims of police violence and how young people had taken to the streets to protest the deaths of Eric Garner, Tamir Rice, Sam DuBose, Sandra Bland, Trayvon Martin, Oscar Grant, Walter Scott, and John Crawford III. I talked about the fact that we needed a president who was willing to listen to the voices of these protestors, to take them seriously, to turn thoughts into action. I wrote about why, as a young Black person in support of the Black Lives Matter movement, I decided to throw my support in Bernie's camp. I talked about the fact that we needed a president who could see that economic and racial inequality were parallel issues, and must be addressed in tandem.

I was proud of the speech. I thought it would hit the right note with the audience, and deliver the message that I wanted, but I'd never written something like this before. So I held my breath as I hit send and emailed it to Jeff Weaver. Just a few hours later, Jeff sent my draft back to me, and there was one edit—in other words, I was right. It was good. I was relieved. But at that point, I had no clue if Bernie or anyone else besides Jeff had read it.

So, I was on my way to Seattle. I was in the air on the plane while two young Black activists interrupted Bernie Sanders while he was giving a speech at a Medicaid event in the city. I saw the video when I landed and looked at the news on my phone. *UGH*, I thought. *What the hell did I just sign up for?* I made my way to the venue. I got to the rally about two hours before we were supposed to walk on stage. The holding area was basically a locker room. There's no makeup, no prep at these kinds of rallies. I got dressed in the women's bathroom.

Then Jeff Weaver came in. "Kid, how are you? Everything good? The senator thinks we should just tell everyone you work here today." I was thinking, *Oh no; here we go.* I was like, "Uh, uh . . . I don't think this is good . . ." I was trying to find a way to say that I don't want to be a token, that I was not on the payroll, that I hadn't been given any training or introduction to the campaign, that it felt like we were kind of flying by the seat of our pants here. But I was also dumbstruck. And then, all of a sudden, I was remembering I still had a job at the trade organization at this point! I hadn't told them I was leaving to work for Bernie Sanders, because they hadn't given me paperwork or a start date! I was struggling to find the words, but it was a major cluster backstage at that point. All the people who were speaking at the rally were swarming around, prepping their lines. I needed to be able to stick up for myself, but everyone was talking, and the ones who were focused on me were assuming I'd do what they wanted.

Then Bernie came in with his wife, Jane. Washington state senator Pramila Jayapal (now a congresswoman) was there too. Bernie came over and was like, "Uh, kiddo . . ." And I was like, "Hi, sir, I'm so happy I'm here . . . but folks are saying I should announce my position today in my speech." He was like, "Yeah, I think that's great." I was like, "I don't know if that's a good idea, sir . . ." Suddenly, everybody was looking at me! It had gone totally silent in the room. I felt very pressured. Because they were pressuring me. It wasn't malicious, but it was like: "Hello, miss, we'd like to tell everyone you work here today."

They wanted to do this for obvious reasons—I'm not stupid. They'd just been harassed by Black activists yet again, and having me go out there and say I'm working on the campaign was an opportunity to change the media narrative; instead of everyone talking about the protestors who interrupted him, they'd be talking about the young press secretary who was also Black that he just hired. They were all just HOPING I would give a good speech. But again: no one had seen my delivery! I was a completely unknown entity at that point—but they liked the way I looked and how I presented myself. And believe me, Bernie was looking at me, Jeff was looking at me, everyone was looking at me, and I thought to myself, *Well, I guess I should just use this to my advantage.* I didn't feel I had many options at that point. So I asked: "Are we telling people I'm the NATIONAL press secretary?" Bernie affirmed this. "Who's introducing me?" I asked. Some tall African American guy—I had no idea who he was at that point—said Senator Jayapal would intro me. Okay. I established, "Just make you say NATIONAL press secretary and my name." And then I agreed.

Then everyone went out to start the rally—there was no turning back. My mind was still racing, wondering whether I'd truly crossed a boundary line for myself personally, whether this was going to ruin my credibility or my reputation. But then I started to calm down and focus. Yes, I was pressured, and I felt pressured. But I'd already said I wanted to work on the campaign. They had already offered me a job, and I had accepted. Was I being used in the moment? Yes, definitely. But I damn well knew I could also use the moment to my own benefit. So then state senator Jayapal introduced me, I walked out onstage, the crowd went crazy, and I went and gave this speech!

I'd like to say I went out there and killed it, but I had never done a crowd that large before. Though I didn't get stage fright, I did feel jittery, and I tend to overcompensate when I get jittery. This was one of the few times in my life I was legitimately nervous. Instead of getting timid or tenuous, I come on strong—the more nerves, the louder the volume. So, in this case (and you can see for yourself; the video is on YouTube), I was absolutely yelling into the mic because I was freaking out a little bit, but I also couldn't hear myself! I wanted to make sure the crowd could hear me and I didn't trust the mic and I'd never done anything like that before.

Now I look at the video, and am like, *I am screaming. Why am I screaming? It's a good speech; I made some excellent points about how young people's voices need to be heard, and I look happy and confident and put-together. But why am I screaming?* So I finished the speech, and then I introed the senator. I heard myself saying, "So please put your hands together for the next president of the United States—Bernie Sanders!" He hugged me on the podium, and then he told me in my ear, "You've definitely got the job." *Whew*, I thought. If the speech had sucked, I wouldn't have gotten the job, so I guess I did okay. Nobody knew if I could do it, and I just did it! I walked off on the little catwalk that led me to the stage, and I stood with some of the other staff to watch Senator Sanders's speech.

Later that evening, I remember getting an email from my mom; she was asking me if I had the same phone number, because she was seeing me on TV and it was all a little bit surreal. I guess she thought maybe now that I was "famous" I'd suddenly have a new phone number. So funny. So exciting. So not true! Things were still totally in start-up mode. For instance, when I got to the hotel in Seattle, I didn't have enough money to pay for the room. I was not getting paid from my regular job at the trade org for a few more days, so I called Jeff Weaver and I was like, "Can someone bring a campaign card to put down for the room so I can check in?" This goes back to what I was saying about how we as women are conditioned to be "nice," to take the burden upon ourselves to be accommodating and accepting. I could have put the charge on my own credit card and kept receipts and tried to get reimbursed and blah, blah, blah, but no. This was a job, which wasn't even really official yet as far as paperwork and all that. I didn't need to be "nice" in this situation. I needed a room. I asked the campaign guy who drove me to the hotel if I could authorize the card for incidentals, "Because I would like to eat. Because I have no money!" He was like, "Okay, and I'll pick you up tomorrow so we can drive to Portland." I'd been asked to go with the team on the rest of the trip from Seattle to Portland to LA—places I'd never been before.

Journos and bloggers and commentators were writing all these articles about the announcement. I was feeling good. But then I realized: *Damn, I really work here!* I needed to figure some things out; I needed to buckle down and learn more about the campaign's inner workings and the issues, and perhaps most important in the moment, why all these activists kept interrupting the senator on the stage and what I could do about it.

So I got on Twitter. I had, like, maybe six hundred followers at that point. I went to DeRay Mckesson's profile—he's a well-known "Black Lives Matter" activist. An activist who specifically made great use of Twitter and social media to get out messages about what was really transpiring on the ground with police violence, in real time. Without Twitter, without social media, no one would have known what was going on as it happened, with both the violence itself and the protests in the aftermath of Michael Brown's death in Ferguson. I decided to look up DeRay on Twitter and send him a direct message. I emailed him, introduced myself, explained that I was working with Bernie now and that I wanted to talk to him about the protesters. I asked if we could talk. DeRay hit me up an hour later, and we talked on the phone for two hours.

I told DeRay right off: my approach is that I'm solutions-oriented. When I was sixteen, I got business cards printed for myself that I used to walk around and give out that said "I specialize in results." Actually, that's still my tagline! In this instance, the result I needed was to open a direct line of communication with these activists and young people who needed to be heard. That was really at the heart of the matter—that's the goal of disruption: it's to get the spotlight focused on you so that your message can be heard, so that it rises above all the distraction and daily life and forces people to pay attention. The other result that I needed was to prevent people from hopping on the stage, interrupting the guy that I now worked for. So I had a great conversation with DeRay, and from there I started to devise a plan. Basically, my approach was to reach out proactively to these activists, in any place we were about to appear, and to set up a listening session with them so they could speak with Bernie directly and air their grievances. In return, they promised not to interrupt his campaign speeches and events.

So, Nick Chedli Carter, Senator Sanders's political outreach director and one of his first campaign hires, picked me up for the drive to Portland. We started talking and he asked, "By the way, why are you here?" So I told him the short version—how I'd gotten the job, how I'd ended up onstage—and he was like, "Damn. That's crazy." As we arrived in Portland, we started hearing reports that activists were planning to interrupt the rally that was planned for that evening. *Okay, here we go,* I thought. I had told Jeff that we needed to find out who was the ringleader of the protests and offer them a sit-down. He and other people on the campaign were skeptical, but I was like, *People are interrupting because they feel like they're not heard, so let's hear them.* But we needed to do that off the record, no press. We needed to reach out. So I asked DeRay: Do you know these folks in Portland? He did! So on the way, I got in touch with a few activists in Portland; Bernie's advance team also reached out to a few contacts. We promised them a meeting after the rally that was coming up; we told them Bernie would sit down with them for a private discussion, but ONLY if they didn't interrupt the event itself.

We arrived at the venue, which was a convention center; we were prepping backstage, and everyone was there— Bernie's advisors, Jeff, campaign staffers, the senator's wife, Jane—and the senator came over in my direction. Then he stopped and announced to all of us that "they" had decided how they'd like to respond to potential protestors. He said: "If we're interrupted tonight, Symone needs to jump in and control the room." Evidently, they wanted me to go up to the mic if there was an interruption and insert myself. I let him explain this plan; I just stood there quietly. I wasn't even on payroll at this point, and I hadn't known any of these people in Bernie's inner circle for more than a matter of days. I cared about their opinions. I cared about my reputation. I don't want to cause trouble. Bernie was also very fired up, which is understandable—who likes to be interrupted and told they're racist on top of that?

When he was done explaining, I asked if he would like my opinion. And in his brusque Bernie voice, he was like, "Sure, sure, whaddaya want?" I said respectfully, "I don't think this is a good idea because the criticism is not of how you are responding to the activists; the criticism is of your supporters—that they don't care enough about issues of race and discrimination and police violence. [We'd established previously that the campaign had a messaging issue.] So if you are telling me you want me to basically shut it down without giving a directive to the crowd on how they should respond, I don't think that bodes well. Also: I'm Black. It will seem like I'm being used for this reason. The optics will be terrible."

He said to me, "We just have a fundamental misunderstanding here," and went on a tangent. I stood firm. "Sir, I get what you want to say; I'm going to get your point across, but I'm going to do it in a way that makes me feel comfortable." He walked away in a huff while others tried to explain, "What he's trying to say is this . . ." In my head I was like, *I know what he's trying to say. You hired me to be your press secretary, not your pep rally girl managing activist logistics.* But then Bernie came back. He'd calmed down, and we agreed to my plan. It was go time.

I walked out onstage and I said this, totally off the cuff: "My name is Symone Sanders, and I have the privilege of serving as the chair of the coalition for juvenile justice's national youth committee. [After this, the juvenile justice committee was like, "Your tenure is over; you can't be using us on the campaign."] I am also joining the campaign this week as the national press secretary. Tonight I have the pleasure of serving as your emcee. Now, I have some good information that there might be the potential for a little disruption tonight. So I wanna be very clear. This campaign is about bringing people together. So if that happens—we hope there won't be a disruption tonight, but if there happens to be a disruption tonight, I want everyone in this stadium to respond with a chant; can y'all do that for me?" The crowd screamed in response that they could. I told them the chant would be "We stand together." And you know what? No one shouted out or rushed the stage. For now.

After the rally, Senator Sanders, Jeff Weaver, communications director Michael Briggs, and I went to a private room for a small discussion that I had arranged, with DeRay's help, with a group of seven or eight activists. As we started the conversation, it was clear that they had been planning on interrupting Bernie's speech before we invited them to speak in this session privately. One of the leaders had been arrested earlier that day, so tensions were high. We sat down for about forty-five minutes, and I moderated the conversation while the young people voiced their concerns. But in reality, I didn't say much. We were there to listen, not to make promises.

These activists wanted to interrupt because they felt that they were not being heard, and as I told Senator Sanders before we went in to meet with them, we can't figure out what they want if we're talking. So we didn't make policy proposals; we simply let them speak, and the senator asked a couple questions. Nowadays, I would be hesitant to throw any candidate or principal into a room like that—where the principal hasn't been briefed, where we don't really know who's coming to the meeting, where anything can happen, really. I was green, I'll admit. Now I would know everything there was to know about a group of people like that before I invited them into a room to talk with my candidate. But at the time, I didn't know much better, and besides, we didn't have the time.

For the next several months, every place we went we reached out to activists in advance. And I'm proud to say that the protests and the heckling stopped. Once I joined the campaign, no one else interrupted the senator while he was onstage. And then, for me, once I got the hang of my role a little bit, I was like, "I don't want to sit behind Bernie Sanders when we're onstage together anymore." I can't be the press secretary if I'm the pep rally girl.

It's good to be impatient, but change does take time. Often, people work for years to achieve a goal, and then it seems to happen overnight because they cross a threshold where their efforts are finally visible. As young as I am, working now for Vice President Biden, I worked on seventeen campaigns, small ones and large ones, before I got to this place.

Big ideas are what move us forward, but incremental steps are sometimes required in order for progress to happen. We cannot wait for a perfect moment, for the stars to align, for the planets to be in step, and THEN take a big leap. Sometimes it's possible, yes. But more often, to achieve the goal of the big idea, we have to get moving in the right direction first. Before we can get to zero emissions by 2050, we have to rejoin the Paris Climate Agreement. A few years ago, saying "universal health coverage" would have prompted immediate and swift lambasting of any candidate who dared utter the words. I was on the campaign trail in a red state in 2014, and believe me, people were not even talking about universal health care "back then," just six years ago. It's clear that we wouldn't be having the conversation about universal health care now without the Affordable Care Act that passed in 2010 (aka Obamacare). People's opinions have changed, but it took time. The majority of Americans now believe health care is a right.

Change takes time, but change also can't wait.

6 STAND IN THE GAP

There's an age-old and well-known Black lady proverb that goes something like this: "Eff it, I'll do it."

Or more elegantly put, in the dedication to their book *For Colored Girls Who Have Considered Politics*, the authors Donna Brazile, Yolanda Caraway, Leah Daughtry, and Minyon Moore wrote the following:

For the women

who ride the early bus
who work the late shift
who teach the children, clean the offices, nurse the sick
who stand guard and keep watch

who build, create, and sustain
who cut new paths and swim in unchartered waters
who light the path and lead the way

who stand up, step up, sit down, and always keep moving
who do the everyday extraordinary work of family,
community, and liberation.

We sing this song for you.

Whether we write poetry or tell jokes about it, it all comes back to the hard fact that so very often, Black women are the ones who have to go in and get things done, go in and have the hard conversations, go in and clean things up after someone makes a mess whether of a political situation (um, hello? More than 90 percent of Black women voted for Clinton in 2016) or a living room. Black women in America have long, perhaps forever, been the cornerstones and the cleaning ladies: the ones who form the foundation and the bedrock of their families and their neighborhoods, the ones who do the domestic laboring that no one else wants to, who do the grief work or grunt work that the country or the community requires.

And you know what? It's exhausting. Black women, though we can, and we do, and we will continue to accomplish things for ourselves, sometimes want a little help. Sometimes we need someone to stand in the gap for us. So many of us who are disenfranchised, or under-supported, or ostracized, or struggling, or misunderstood, or outcast need accomplices, not just allies. Society needs people who are willing to stand up for one another and step in for one another. We need to learn to stand in the gap, to close the space so other people can make it over to the land of opportunity, which right now is unreachable, no matter how hard they work, how much they lean in, or how far they leap.

Here's the problem with asking people to stand in the gap for others. People don't like to be uncomfortable. But think about. If you can choose to avoid discomfort, you're already way better off than many other folks out there. You can choose to turn away from discrimination or racism because you don't want to see it. Some people wake up uncomfortable because they haven't eaten a proper meal in days, or they're worried about getting evicted, or they're living on the street with their kids, or they're working three jobs to pay the bills. It's tough for people to embody or internalize: How do I really use my power to stand up for someone else?

When I think about standing in the gap, I think about Heather Heyer. Heather was a young woman who went out to a counter-protest in Charlottesville on August 12, 2017, to oppose the white supremacists who had gathered in the city to rally. She was killed for her convictions and her refusal to back down in the face of racism. Heather Heyer was not Black, she was not a person of color, she was not Jewish, she was not a member of any group of people that the neo-Nazis or the white supremacists were there talking about. But Heather went out to stand in the gap.

She wasn't just an ally to those who were being attacked by the Unite the Right folks—she was more than that. She was an accomplice. Me, I don't want more allies. Because sometimes your ally has an alibi, a get-out-of-jail-free card. They're with you, beside you, until the going gets tough. An accomplice doesn't have an easy out. An accomplice goes out there with you, takes risks the same as you. Heather was an accomplice, so much so that she lost her life standing in the gap. I am not suggesting that folks need to or should run out and lay down their lives for social justice. But there are real, tangible opportunities to stand in the gap for others. It leads back to the idea that we have to be radical revolutionaries in our everyday spaces and places. We don't take these opportunities. Because it makes us uncomfortable.

It's uncomfortable work to speak up. I'll say that sometimes, I just want to go to my job. I don't want to be the Black girl at the office. Sometimes I just wanted to show up in class; I didn't want to be the person that people looked at to provide them with teachable moments. It's uncomfortable to speak up, to ask people to do something they haven't done before, to buck the status quo.

Let me tell you about one super-uncomfortable situation in 2016, when I found myself way out there in the gap, looking for someone to grab on to. It was early on the campaign trail in 2016, but it was one of the times when we had Secret Service and the good plane. When things are going well, you've got money, you're riding a good wave, then the plane is nice and you've got hot meals and liquor any time you want. This is in a good spell of campaign life, which could come to an abrupt and screeching halt at any moment. You know the moment is over when you go from the good plane to an old plane, you don't have Wi-Fi, and you're eating boxed lunches with cold-cut sandwiches and stale chips. That day is always near.

But at this point we were riding high. It was the first rally of the new year in 2016. I had a poppin' peacoat from Banana Republic. We arrived at a large venue in Massachusetts to a packed crowd; it was a school auditorium, and there was not enough room, so we went outside beforehand so the senator could briefly address the overflow crowd—about two hundred people that couldn't get in. So we went outside, I introduced the senator, everyone was all excited, and then he spoke. I was standing just off to the side with a senior advisor; our trip director, who was a tall African American man named Paul; our campaign manager; and maybe one other person. Bernie finished; we were ready to go into the building to do our rally, the thing we came to do.

We were all feeling good after warming up the crowd outside. The entrance to the building was just about a hundred feet away, and as we started walking in the direction of the doors, I heard someone yelling, "Ma'am. Ma'am! Move to the side! Move!" I was like, *Dang, that lady they're yelling at better move.* Next thing I know, a state trooper had his hands on me; he was yanking me out of Senator Sanders's entourage. I was walking next to Paul, who threw his arm over me, stopped everyone else with his other hand outstretched, and said to the trooper, "Do we have a problem? This is the national press secretary." The state trooper went, "Uh, I'm sorry. I didn't know." And I looked at him and said, "Because the Black girl couldn't be with Bernie Sanders, right?" And then I turned around to the senator, who'd been held up by the commotion and was looking on aghast, and I said, "This is what I'm always talking about." As I calculated my next move, Paul looked at me. He gave me this calm stare and said, "What are we going to do?" and I said, "We've got work to do." He said, "Not going to let the devil get us." "Not today," I said. And so Paul and I walked into the event venue, everybody else followed after. But throughout that whole exchange, nobody but Paul said *anything.* I don't know that anyone except Paul or myself will even remember that story today, but it is forever seared into my brain because I needed somebody to have my back. I needed somebody to speak up for me. And I'm sure it was really uncomfortable for Paul. But he had my back. And I don't think that the other folks in the entourage didn't speak up because they felt what the state trooper was doing was acceptable. I don't think they didn't speak up because they agreed with the assumptions at work. I think they didn't speak up because it was uncomfortable. They didn't speak up because they weren't ready to be accomplices.

There will be times where you have an opportunity to stand in the gap, to speak up for somebody, but it makes you uncomfortable. And you don't move, don't act, don't say something. Part of being a radical revolutionary is stepping in on that homophobic joke, being willing to say something when someone comes up saying something racist, even if that person is someone close to you, someone you never expected to hold those kinds of views.

In a speech on the Vietnam War, delivered on April 4, 1967, exactly one year before his assassination, Dr. King said, "A time comes when silence is betrayal." We have to be willing to speak up, to be uncomfortable. Part of being a radical revolutionary and standing in the gap means being able to engage in uncomfortable conversations. We live in a culture right now where we can choose to isolate ourselves in echo chambers with people who think like us, look like us, vote like us. There's literally a button on Facebook that says *hide all content like this* so you never have to see anything that you do not like. We are living in a culture where we are hiding all content like this in our everyday spaces and places. We are refusing to engage with the world and with others in our real-life human interactions, to the point where we don't even know how to have uncomfortable conversations with people, let alone stand up and put ourselves at risk for people who aren't like us. People are avoided and left out of the conversation every day, in boardrooms, in communities, in politics, and it takes the collective "we" to step in and stand up. Otherwise people will keep doing it.

Here's an uncomfortable truth I hold: I believe that we have yet to have a real conversation about race or equity in America because the conversation has yet to be had outside of the lens of white supremacist ideology and the patriarchy. And let's not think that people of color and women don't perpetuate these systems every single day; we have all internalized it. When a Black person tells another person of color, "You talk white," that's white supremacist ideology speaking right there: the idea that a Black person is trying to be something they aren't when they use a certain vocabulary or diction. Or when women during the Kavanaugh hearings said, "I wouldn't want my son to be treated the way that Kavanaugh is being treated during this trial"—well, wait a minute! Would your son be in that position, where Kavanaugh found himself, if he hadn't been drunk and pinning down a girl on a bed? Maybe some of my viewers and fans don't want to hear that, but backing down or watering down my beliefs, just because they're upsetting to some, doesn't change the truth behind them. I wake up every day determined to tell the truth no matter how uncomfortable it may make some.

I take my work as a political operative seriously. A battle is being waged in this country, and eventually it will be over. I don't want to sit on the sidelines. Because when it ends, we have to ask ourselves: Where do we find ourselves now? Have we helped to create solutions, improve lives? Are we all better off than we were before? Are Black people, young people, women, LGBTQ+ folks in a better position? I hope that we can say that the work we are doing in our communities matters, that when the battle is done being waged, we sit in a better position. That requires some real work. That requires us to be radical revolutionaries. That requires us to do some things that have not been done before. It requires us to stand in the gap for one another, but to know that doesn't give anyone an exemption from behaving with integrity. The work that happened fifty years ago colors the lives we are able to lead today. The work we are doing right now will dictate the quality and nature of people's lives fifty years from now.

For instance, I've learned what I have about standing in the gap, and I am able to be where I am today because of people like the women who wrote the poem at the start of this chapter. This group of badass Black women at the upper echelons of American politics call themselves the Colored Girls. They are Donna Brazile, a total shero of mine, who you know by now and who also happens to be a political commentator and the first Black woman to direct a major presidential campaign; Minyon Moore, who was director of White House political affairs under President Clinton and former CEO and chief operating officer of the Democratic National Committee; Yolanda Caraway, a public affairs and relations specialist who was chief of staff of the National Rainbow Coalition and the 1988 Jesse Jackson presidential campaign, and deputy chair of the DNC; and Leah Daughtry, a reverend who was the CEO of the 2016 and 2008 Democratic National Convention and chief of staff to Howard Dean. They in turn got to where they are because of people like Reverend Willie T. Barrow and Congresswoman Eleanor Holmes Norton, who came before and stood in the gap so they could cross over to greater successes.

Willie T. Barrow was born into a family of seven kids in a small town in Texas in 1924. She started her lifelong involvement in activism early, when she organized a protest at age twelve to argue for the right of Black students to ride the bus to school. She grew into a national civil rights leader despite her small stature of four foot eleven, which earned her the nickname "Little Warrior." Barrow worked with Reverend King in the 1950s as a field organizer for the Southern Christian Leadership Conference; she organized and participated in the Selma and Washington marches of the 1960s. With Reverend Jesse Jackson, she helped create Operation Breadbasket, which became Operation PUSH (People United to Serve Humanity), and later served on Jackson's presidential campaigns. In the

'80s, she succeeded Jesse Jackson as executive director of Operation PUSH, and in the '90s she continued her life-long practice of standing in the gap when she went out there supporting the LGBT community and fighting for HIV/AIDS victims. She became godmother to Barack Obama—and to nearly one hundred other people too—and a national icon. She did so by recognizing that she couldn't, and didn't want to, do the work alone. In the civil rights era, "I opened my house up to all the powerful women in the movement—Coretta Scott King, Dorothy Height, Addie Wyatt," she told the *Chicago Sun-Times*. "That's how I learned." In her later years, she observed, "We have to teach this generation . . . [we must] train more Corettas, more Addies, more Dorothys. If these young people don't know whose shoulders they stand on, they'll take us back to slavery. And I believe that's why the Lord is still keeping me here." She tirelessly worked for the rights of the oppressed until she died in 2015, at the age of ninety.

Another trailblazing figure still doing the work is Congresswoman Eleanor Holmes Norton. Congresswoman Norton was born in Washington, DC, in 1937, the daughter of a teacher and a civil servant. While at Antioch College she became an organizer for the Student Nonviolent Coordinating Committee and organized and participated in sit-ins. As a student at Yale Law School, she joined in the Mississippi Freedom Summer and worked with activists including Medgar Evers and Fannie Lou Hamer. She became a stalwart advocate for civil rights and women's rights: she served as assistant legal director of the American Civil Liberties Union, the first female chair of the U.S. Equal Employment Opportunity Commission, appointed by President Jimmy Carter, and professor at Georgetown University Law Center before being elected to the House of Representatives in 1990, where she still serves, now as a Democratic superdelegate.

These women are just a few of the people who enabled me to get where I am today. I owe it to them and to the activists and revolutionaries and operatives coming up now to continue to stand in the gap for others. But while standing up and acting on behalf of other people, you also need to look out for yourself. Because you are not going to be a good accomplice, radical revolutionary, or even friend if you aren't feeling good about what you yourself are doing. A big part of this is being honest with yourself about your long-term goals, and also reclaiming your time from all of the forces that want to pull it away from you, toward frivolous or meaningless or unfulfilling stuff. The first step for me is understanding what it is I want to do, short term and long term, and then making commitments that will hold me to those goals.

Oftentimes we can't seize opportunities because we're not clear on what we actually WANT to do, and so we end up doing random things and a year or five or ten years later you're like, *Why I am over HERE doing THIS at this company?*

I was supposed to be over THERE by now . . . wherever that may be. Maybe you're making more money than you once thought possible, but you're not fulfilled or the work itself lacks meaning. Maybe your family life sucks because you come home at ten p.m. every night and can't spend time with your partner or your kids. Or maybe you've never taken a risk and gone in pursuit of that dream job that would pay you well to do what you like. Perhaps you've lost track of your best friends, all because you didn't take time to sustain your friendships when your career took off. We can't be our authentic selves if we don't know who we as- pire to become. If you're not your authentic self, you can't get to the place where you want to be. This goes back to my advice earlier about writing down your goals. It sounds small, but writing it down and expressing it is what makes it real! You can't say it as a joke either: part of being pre- pared for an opportunity is taking it seriously. It's an im- portant step to take at a time when you can think with a clear head and create a vision for your future. Because sometimes people will push you off track, sometimes you'll meander aimlessly for too long, and sometimes life comes along and smacks you to the ground.

That's what happened to me on March 18, 2017, when my father died suddenly. He had a stroke while he was working out at the gym, back home in Omaha, and two weeks later he was gone. I didn't take time off to process what happened, or to be with my family, and I should have. The day after his memorial service I was doing a speaking engagement; two days later I was back on TV. But inside, and in my life beyond the cameras, I was not well.

Things finally came to a head on my birthday in December 2017. I had a party at a fancy lounge place in DC. I didn't reserve it exclusively because the party was supposed to be twenty friends; one hundred people showed up. I don't remember too many specifics about that night, but I can remember that I caused a scene. The police came. I remember leaving the venue with coat over my head and being like, "TAKE ME OUT OF HERE; THEY'RE TAKING MY PICTURE!" Weeping, absolutely a mess.

The next day, one of my best friends was like, "You know, you were out of control yesterday." I replied, ridiculously: "I wasn't out of control." He insisted: "You were. You need to think a little bit about how you've been acting this year." Again, I was like, *UGH. THE AUDACITY!* A week later, my good girlfriends at the party—the ones who later kept me off the venue's official blacklist, and also made sure I had my keys and got my passport that night as I was escorted out of the place—took me to dinner and hosted their own sensitive intervention. They said, "You've had a tough year. But you need to pull back. You're running around the town and the country, traveling, hanging out, turning up everywhere. We're concerned that something is going to happen that will have lasting implications."

Instead of quiet time when I was off camera and off

work, I was going out, jumping on a plane and traveling to Miami, partying too hard. Here's something to know about me: I will take the party from zero to one hundred in the first five minutes. (Just as I can take the interview from zero to one hundred in the first five minutes.) I wasn't dealing well with the loss of my dad. I was worried about how my mom and my siblings were managing, but I was also avoiding going home. My sister's college graduation had been two months after my father's passing, and it was so incredibly tough to go to an event like that and not have him there. What made it more difficult was all of the people telling me they were sorry for my loss and that they missed my dad. People would see me out in town and come up and say these things, which I knew came from a good place, but I felt crippled talking about it at the time. I didn't want to go home again for a while after that. This was the first time I'd experienced such a profound loss. My mother always puts on a brave face and powers through, but I know it was difficult for her, and still is.

Now, through prayer and therapy, I can talk about my father freely, but I'll admit, I'm a crier, and just thinking about all of this makes me tear up. What people don't tell you is that when you have a loss like that in your life, your sadness never leaves you. You learn to move through it. When I got the opportunity to work on the Biden campaign, I was sad when I thought about the fact that my dad would never know it. I get sad thinking about how my dad won't see this book come out, or be there to walk me down the aisle, or that if I have kids they won't get to know him. He doesn't get to share in the experience of the great things I plan to do with my life. But you know what? I'm also grateful. I'm happy. I am happy that I'm coping and dealing with it and that I'm moving forward. I know that the best way I can honor my father is to continue to do what I'm doing—to go full steam ahead on the things that I believe in, to work my tail off to make change where I can. But in the immediate aftermath of losing my dad, I did not deal well. I didn't take the time to get the help I needed, on top of all this professional stuff like having my own consulting business and working with Priorities USA and showing up on the regular on CNN.

One of my mentors, Tanya Lombard, an executive at AT&T who used to work with Minyon Moore, also sat me down for a come to Jesus. She took me out to dinner and she said to me, "Look, I lost my father when I was young, so I know what it feels like. But you've got a lot going on, so you can't do this. You need help in order to really deal with this, Symone. You cannot act out. And you cannot let grief consume you."

I was so defensive at first: I insisted that my friends who cared about me didn't understand what it was like to always have people on your back. The loss of my dad came at a time just as people were really starting to recognize me. I was struggling with that loss of privacy, that feeling of becoming a public persona that had to behave in a certain way. I also felt like my friends didn't understand that pressure to perform. It was new to me—I'd been doing TV since the campaign, but I was a pundit by the end of 2017. I was grateful that Tanya cared, and that she took the time to check up on me, but I also wasn't ready to confront the bigger issues she brought up.

So when Tanya and other mentors and friends were sitting me down in February 2018, my response was a whiny "YOU DON'T KNOW MY LIIIIIIIFE!" But their message finally came through—and they were so right. I needed to get myself together. I had no idea that I was so stressed and overwhelmed and also grief-stricken. I had to deal with the newfound responsibilities of my platform at the same time. The latter, I think, is something that happens to most people throughout their lives, even if you're not on TV—any time you move up, when you can reach things you hadn't been able to access before, all of a sudden you're buying stuff you couldn't afford before, showing up at important meetings even though you're not really focused or emotionally prepared; maybe you're a bit loose and maxed out.

I got to that point. I woke up to the fact that I needed to be more in control, needed to better manage myself. I committed to regularly going to a therapist, and I felt a sense of calmness and relaxation that I hadn't felt before. I'm so grateful that big-sister figures like Tanya cared enough about me to call me and check up on me and question my behavior. My mom calls and checks on me because she's supposed to. Tanya doesn't have to—but she did, and she does. People like her are a good reminder that in doing this work, in creating space for change, we also have to remember to be good stewards of relationships. We can't be so entrenched in the work that we forget to be good people, and to help one another. And we'll also get a lot further a lot faster if we stand in the gap for one another along the way.

My life went from zero to sixty right around this time—I made HUGE professional leaps. While I felt I'd done the work to be prepared professionally, these leaps came really fast, and I wasn't prepared to deal with the by-products of that emotionally. Even if it's not about public exposure or how you behave in public, most people will have to make strategic decisions about how their personal behavior intersects with their career and professional life at some point. You may find you have to make personal sacrifices.

It's easier sometimes just to go along a certain path— perhaps it's the path of least resistance or it's the path that you feel was set out for you by societal pressure to achieve a certain income, or family expectations to go into a certain line of work. For me, when I joined the Biden campaign as senior advisor, some people were aghast. They were like, *You're a traitor to Bernie and the causes that he supports*—a traitor to millennials, essentially—and all kinds of other stuff.

I will forever respect Senator Sanders for taking a

chance on me. I was like, "I want to be national press secretary," and he basically said, *Cool. I'll give you a shot.* But I scoff at the idea that I should be expected to forever toe the line, when the nature of our relationship was he took a chance on me, and I took a chance on him. Look, nobody talked me through the talking points—matter of fact, there weren't any, so I wrote them myself. Nobody taught me how to gaggle with reporters. I figured that out by trial and error, and sometimes it was ugly. So now that I've come on board with the Biden campaign, I find it audacious that anyone demand that I be loyal to somebody that ain't necessarily going to be loyal to me. People would not be telling me the same things if I were a thirty-five-year-old white man.

But I'm confident in the direction I've chosen. My values are not tied to a particular person. My values are tied to what it is that I believe, not wrapped up in some political personality. For folks that really want to go out and change the apparatus, people that want to remake the system, you have to have some solid core values. That sounds like common sense, but in reality I think that's a problem for many people who get involved in politics. They get it twisted and they find their values are wrapped up in Obama, in Bernie Sanders, in Joe Biden, in some other political persona. I have immense respect for all three of those people, but my values are not wrapped up in any one of them. I didn't go to work for Bernie because I was a die-hard Bernie fan. I went to work for him because the things he was talking about at the time and the way he was talking about them aligned with my values for the most part. And I asked for a particular job—basically I demanded a seat at the table—and they gave me the seat I asked for. That seat put me in a position to do real change-making work, and to put my career on the trajectory I wanted.

PIECE OF ADVICE

CLEAR SPACE FOR YOUR GOALS

Freedom isn't easily attained, and no one is going to hand you the next level of freedom—by that I mean financial freedom or more time off or the freedom to do more of what you want in your day-to-day work life. You have to figure out how to demand what you need, and make the time for what you want. We are ALL busy, but we must make time for things we consider valuable. So if addressing poverty is important to you, make time for it! Give your time to a group that is working to combat poverty in your community or one nearby. If you want to improve the educational system . . . make time for it. Figure out how to join the school board or run for office in your school district.

*You want local organic lettuce in your neigh-
borhood grocery store . . . make time for it! Go
talk to the vendors and suppliers at your local
farmers' markets. Voting is one of the neces-
sary tools in the toolbox of social justice, but
voting isn't enough. I say pick ONE thing in
addition to voting and do that. You don't have
to start from scratch, and you don't need to do
it alone. There are other like-minded people
out there already doing the work. Make it your
mission to find and join them.*

I didn't 110 percent agree with Bernie on every issue
while I was working for him. I don't agree with Biden on
every issue, in every instance. But I think in order to make
change we have to make strategic decisions. That's not
sexy. Nobody wants to talk about it. No one wants to make
choices or sacrifices or do the grunt work, but somebody's
gotta transcribe what was said, somebody has to run secu-
rity, someone has to book the travel, and someone's gonna
be up till two a.m. the night before a debate, reviewing and
reviewing and rereviewing talking points. People don't talk
about how many times Whitney M. Young Jr. or James
Farmer or John Lewis or other people from what's known
as the Big Six (a group of civil rights leaders who helped
mastermind and steer the movement) had to run around
behind the scenes in the White House, talking to other

people, the policy makers, not to mention staff assistants, schedulers, and all of that while Dr. King was talking to the president. Or how King then had to go back and talk to the business community after bartering with the president, be a broker between everybody, and try to convince people to change their minds and their practices. You have to be strategic. Dr. King didn't just give a good speech, wave his hand, and say, "All right, now change is gonna come." Get the heck up out of here.

You can't achieve anything good if you aren't standing in the gap for somebody else. Those other people need to hear your voice in solidarity with theirs. And working to continue in the spirit of those that came before us, we need people that are committed to shifting the status quo, using all means and methods at our disposal.

7

DON'T TAKE NO FOR AN ANSWER

(BUT DO YOUR HOMEWORK FIRST)

I n the age of radical revolutionary work, if we are going to truly accomplish anything, we need to believe in ourselves. Young people, melanated people, differently abled people: if we are out there doing the work, showing that we are prepared, showing that we take ourselves and our ability to create change seriously, other people will start to take us more seriously as well. It's not always easy to feel confident about what you are doing, especially when society at large might question you or your tactics or motives, but it gets a lot simpler if we start by supporting and standing up for one another. This will help us as individuals to become more confident in our skills and knowledge and what we have to offer.

I joined Bidenworld as a total newbie to that particular, peculiar scene. Yes, I have lots of experience doing campaign work at this point, and I've done plenty of political commentating. But I've never worked on a presidential campaign this early in the process, I've never worked in the White House before (as most of Biden's staff and advisors have), and perhaps most important, I had not previously been involved in Biden's forty-plus-year career in the public sphere. A good number of the people working with and around him were there when he introduced and sponsored the Violence Against Women Act in 1990, or when he helped push the Brady Bill and the assault weapons ban through the Senate in 1994.

All of that is true, but it also doesn't mean I have no place being involved in his campaign. I'm a young, intelligent, well-spoken Black woman who has already served as a national press secretary for a leading presidential candidate, a paid regular contributor on CNN, a political pundit and commentator, and a juvenile justice advocate. I know firsthand the bravery, dedication, and commitment it takes to clap back at existing power structures. I didn't get to this place alone. I've had my self-doubts along the way. I've also gained a lot of confidence from the people around me who have supported and encouraged me. And perhaps most important, I've learned not to give a you-know-what when someone tells me no.

We cannot afford to stop at the *no*. Because you're going to hear a lot of nos if you are out there trying to change the way power works in our country, if you are standing up as an ally for others, if you are challenging the status quo. I believe you need to push back EVERY SINGLE TIME someone denies that which you know you have worked for and deserve. If you believe it is yours, if you believe that it is due to you, don't let anybody tell you that you can't have it. Do not let others define the terms of your life for you. Do not let others tell you that because it's always been done a certain way in the past, or has never been done by someone "like you," that you need to step back. That's exactly when to press forward.

I have heard from people who question my role in the political sphere at this level entirely—and I don't mean the haters, who I just dismiss out of hand. I mean people like the young Black woman who heard me give a keynote at her university, and then tweeted about how she couldn't believe the direction that I chose to pursue in my career. "Symone Sanders out here talking a big game about being a radical revolutionary and then joins the Biden campaign. What??" She's not the only one; plenty of people come up to me or ask me online: How can you be talking about the revolution and Black people and go talk to Biden? I am at a place in my career where I can really influence not only the conversation, but also the direction and outcome. I know people might not think what I'm doing is radical or revolutionary, but you know what? It IS radical and revolutionary that I have an opportunity to be as involved as I am in the making of a president. We are literally in the process of creating and choosing our next president in the wake of the tenure of one of the most disastrous leaders we have ever elected. We need to stop demonizing people for going to work on the inside of the apparatus or taking a job at a certain company or whatnot—we're always talking about "Where are the Black women?" or "Where are the young people?" or "Where are the women?" and then the moment somebody shows up or steps up, we criticize them for where they stepped up to.

I gave up a lot of money for a lot more stress when I walked away from my solid salary—which I earned while literally sitting on TV, where I was getting my makeup done every day, perched in a comfortable air-conditioned studio, talking to interesting people, and getting to share my opinion with a large audience—to go bust my tail flying all over the country to big cities, small towns, and everywhere in between, putting in eighteen-hour days, in order to work for a candidate that I believe can make a real difference for the world. I walked away from being able to brunch on the weekends because I wanted to go be effective. Because I wanted to contribute. In the end, I really like doing the operative stuff, the behind-the-scenes communication work. Because that's where the real work is and the decisions are made.

I got into politics because I wanted to make a difference. That's it. And on that journey to make a difference, I figured out that politics was nothing more than a bunch of messages people strung together—usually while sitting around a table—and then they dictate to other people how they want that message delivered. A campaign is just repeating that message over and over again in various communities across the country, or within a state, a district, or a city, and convincing those people to be with you on what you are saying. The comms people, whether it's on a campaign or in a high-level meeting about a company's message, always get to sit at the table, and I knew that. But at the same time, the people at that table didn't look like me—they weren't young, they weren't Black, and they weren't women. And then it hit me the other day. We were sitting at a table in a conference room, doing a senior strategy session with staff and senior advisors. I looked around and realized, THIS was the freaking table I was always talking about! It blew my mind. I zoned out for a minute just thinking about that. Most people work their whole careers to be able to sit at that table and make those decisions. Now I'm there, at twenty-nine. And I'm not going to waste a second of my opportunity to be there, or listen to anyone who says I don't belong or that I've somehow "sold out" by being part of the political process, by joining Biden's campaign.

One of the important questions I really want to answer before the next election is lofty: Why does the Democratic Party's messaging seem to not be working in some places? Where is it failing, falling short? My feeling is some people perceive that the party is too concerned with *telling* the voters how they can keep the American experiment intact without focusing on *what* we the people are actually saying we want to change about our democracy. The message put out by the apparatus is: *we will help you, we know best, we have the answer.* But the American people, those who make up the factions of the Democratic Party, are tired of this.

Individuals from many different classes, ethnicities, races, genders, and background experiences have all concluded that they no longer want to hear empty promises. They want to see their fellow Americans speaking, and the leaders of the Democratic Party listening: they want to see Parkland students giving speeches on gun control, and congressmen and -women taking action. The wants of the people need to lead in this new age. If the Democratic Party makes this its aim, the factions on the ground will not work against the apparatus in Washington, DC. If the apparatus stops *telling* and *asks* the people to construct what the party should be saying, the party will see a brighter future.

Now, there is a belief among progressive people, and definitely among some young people, particularly those under the age of forty, that you have to be 110 percent on board to sign up for something. If it doesn't meet all twenty things on your checklist, then you don't do it? I think that's unrealistic at best and lazy at worst. Just because doing something doesn't check all twenty of your boxes of what you want to accomplish, all at once, that doesn't mean you sit around and do nothing or wait for something to change before you take action. Because as I talked about earlier on, in order to change the apparatus we have to have access to it first. How can I best effect real change in the world? How can I truly make a difference? These are the questions I ask myself when people accuse me of not keeping it real.

Speaking of keeping it real and staying true to yourself, of course I have moments of doubt when it comes to knowing myself while others question me. Sometimes, my vision gets cloudy and I second-guess my capabilities or what I should do next to be as effective as I can be. One day in the spring of 2016, I thought I was going to walk off the Bernie campaign because I no longer felt valued and I tired of people questioning my skills and commitment—some inside the campaign, and some people in the media and outside of the campaign too. When I joined, people thought I had no campaign experience, no political experience, and that I'd literally been plucked out of obscurity. Nah. I'd worked on fifteen campaigns before I got to Bernie. No, never for a potential presidential nominee, but still, I'd worked on fifteen other campaigns. I remember early on, someone in-house told me over email that I could answer if BET or

Telemundo came calling, but if the *Washington Post* or *NYT* called, I should forward any requests to him. I remember drafting my email back, deleting and rewriting and deleting and emailing so that I didn't sound totally furious. In the end, I think I went with something like: "Thank you, but as the national press secretary I believe I'm empowered to speak to ALL press!"

In April 2016, Donna Brazile and Nina Turner both called me to check in and see how I was doing. When I started complaining about the situation, they each gave me the tough love I needed. I'll never forgot Donna had all the questions (and the answers): "Are they threatening to fire you?" No. "Are you still getting paid?" Yes. "Do you have another job lined up?" No. "Then WHAT ARE YOU DOING? Get up and go to work; pull it together! What is wrong with you? We will help you, but you have got to get back to work." Sometimes you need the people around you telling YOU no! (Get it together, folks!) You need people you trust who you know will pull you back when they see you wandering off track. Sometimes we get into spaces and places with a lot of yes people. There are scores of them in politics. I don't want any yes people. And I sure as hell won't be anyone else's yes woman.

But I did still need to trust my own sense of direction in my career. And that's how I arrived at the decision when I knew it was a time for me to leave the Sanders campaign. In the summer of 2016, things were getting bitter as it became more and more clear that Secretary Clinton was the presumptive nominee, and yet Sanders refused to concede. It caused a lot of rancor within the Democratic Party, and I started to feel uncomfortable for my role in perpetuating it. The race was definitely over, but I stayed through all the nominating contests because I believed what Bernie was saying—that everyone should be able to cast their ballot for the candidate of their choosing. The day before the California primary, the Associated Press had already called the race for Secretary Clinton. The polls weren't even open, and they said, "Sorry, folks, it's over." Ha! And of course they were right. We lost. So, now what? Bernie was going to continue on; that much was clear. But it was also becoming evident that it was time for me to go.

I had been "living" in Burlington, Vermont, since September of 2015 since that's where the Sanders campaign was headquartered. I didn't actually spend a ton of time in Burlington, but I did have an apartment there that I would go back to when I wasn't on the trail. A few weeks before the California primary, my lease on the Vermont apartment was up. I knew I wasn't going to renew it; I knew my time was coming to a close on the campaign, but I wasn't quite sure how to extricate myself. So I went and packed up my stuff, managed to cram it all in a car, and I drove to DC. I crashed at my mom's friend Lorna's place, assuring her that it was temporary. (HA! More on that in a minute . . .) Anyway, I put my stuff at Lorna's house, and then I went off to California for the primary on June 7. We got our tails handed to us. There's a picture of me and the deputy communications director and the deputy press secretary out at breakfast the next morning with our heads down, all staring at our phones and notes, looking tired, but ready to press on.

A little later that month, I went to a bipartisan political conference in LA called Politicon. I hadn't officially quit the campaign. I had given my two weeks to Jeff Weaver, but no one else knew. In advance of the convention, someone in the Sanders campaign had sent out a statement about the Democratic committee platform, and I hadn't seen it. So we were at Politicon and reporters in the greenroom started whispering and then talking openly about it, and they started coming right up to me, asking for comments. I was like, "We don't have a statement." And they were like, "Yes, you do." Me: "No, we don't." Them: "Yes, you do." I asked one of the reporters who was being especially persistent to let me read the statement on his phone. Okay, fine. There it was. Right then and there I called up the head of the communications department and told them I was done. I called Jeff Weaver and told him that I was going to let everyone else know I was leaving. I emailed Bernie and Mrs. Sanders to thank them for the ride of a lifetime. Then I walked out onstage. The emcee introed me as press secretary for Bernie, and right then and there I corrected them: "*Former* press secretary for Bernie Sanders."

My mom called. "Symone, your name is scrolling on the bottom of CNN. Did they fire you?" I didn't freak out; I just calmly told her, "No, Madre, I quit!" And I didn't second-guess myself. I didn't feel like I was making the wrong choice—not for one second. After so much craziness on the campaign trail and the nonstop action of keeping up and keeping ahead and always being on call and responding to every piece of news or every request from the senator, I felt at peace for the first time in months. Stepping off the campaign at that point was what I needed to do, for myself and for my career.

When I left the Sanders campaign in 2016, I thought I was going to work on the Hillary campaign. I remember going to Brooklyn one afternoon and folks assuring me it was pretty much a done deal. All I needed to do was wait for a call from someone in the communications department the following week. Welp, the call never came, so that was a clear NO. I was, however, still doing television during this time and quickly realized I was going to the studio for free while other folks were getting paid. So I figured the place where I could continue to truly help give voice to the movement and a lift to my bank account so I could at least pay my phone bill was on TV. But it wasn't as if I just walked off the campaign trail and onto the set. Oh, no, no, no. Speaking of *no*, I got so many nos from agents and other leads that I lost count, but I wasn't going to let that stop me. Back when I started with Bernie, first

I had to convince the campaign people that I belonged in front of the camera. Because the same person that believed I should only speak to BET and Telemundo couldn't fathom I could be a credible on-air spokesperson. Even six months after I joined, it was still really hard to be allowed to do part of the job I was hired for. Frankly, I think I owe my entire TV career to Tad Devine and Poppy Harlow. Tad believed in me, advocated for me, and is the reason the hater on the communications team was overruled. Meanwhile, Poppy Harlow of CNN, who used to anchor Saturday afternoons, was an advocate for putting women in front of the camera. While other shows and networks would literally tell our bookers they wanted "the big dogs," aka Tad and Jeff Weaver, Poppy's team would regularly throw my name in the mix as a campaign spokesperson they would like to have on. Poppy valued my voice as an equal contributor to my male counterparts. I will always be grateful she said yes.

Okay, back to life post–Sanders campaign. I had a lot of big ideas, but I also had no money and no job. I'd been doing some regular spots on TV by this point, which all my friends thought was cool, but I didn't have a contract, so I wasn't getting paid, and not to mention I was BROKE. Something they don't teach in college (and you sure don't get a class in while on the campaign trail) is financial literacy. My lease was up; I'd totaled my car. I needed help. One of my mom's sorority sisters, Lorna, offered to let me stay at her house (more like was backed into a corner and reluctantly said yes) while I looked for a job. I took this as an opportunity to go full millennial mooch off someone who wasn't even a blood relation.

So here's the backstory: It was May 2016. I texted Lorna (I didn't even call—such a millennial) to ask if I could stay in her house for a little while. I think I framed it in some vague manner like: *Can I put my items in the guest room?* She texts back, *Yes.* I said it was only gonna be two to three months. After that I ended up working on the Democratic National Convention, where I essentially made up a job for myself as a consultant. So I went to Philly for a while, but was back at her house end of July. I still didn't have a *job* job—I didn't have a network contract, so I was working for free trying to figure out my next move. And in the meantime, I was hanging out with friends, coming home at three a.m. on a Tuesday—to the very loud sound of the garage door going up and down and waking Lorna, who had a very demanding job as an energy lobbyist.

I'm ashamed to admit it, but I was acting more like a brat than a radical revolutionary. What's worse: I wasn't paying for anything—no groceries, no rent, no utilities, nothing. I'd get Uber Eats and sometimes would not offer to get her anything! I did introduce Lorna to the wonderful world of takeout and Rice Krispies treats from Costco, though! In other words, I was twenty-six years old acting like a fifteen-year-old. Fast-forward: it was November 2016;

days were dismal. I didn't come home for four days. I was just hanging out with friends! Donald Trump just got elected! I couldn't deal! Finally, Lorna texted me and was like, "I need to talk to you." Ugh. Sometimes Lorna was my big sis; sometimes she was my other mother.

She went right into it, said, "I want to know what your plan is." I told her: "I've been saving a bit, so my plan is to stay here until March, and I think I'll have enough to pay rent at a place of my own. Then I'm gonna look to get another contract . . ." She said, "I want you to think about this a little more."

Over the next month, it became clear that my leaving in March was not soon enough. We had another conversation. Lorna went, "You millennials"—already irksome—"think you can do whatever it is you want to do and be whoever it is you want to be. You've been told that your whole lives, but it won't always be like this. The life you're living now, it won't always be like this."

Of course, this is great food for thought. But at the time I was thinking (not, thank God, SAYING): *She's trying to kill my dreams! She doesn't understand.* I responded, "I hear you, Lorna. I'll be out in January." I had nowhere to live, and I hadn't been looking. I went on Craigslist and found a place that I could move into in three weeks. I told Lorna, and she was like, "Oh, what is it?" I said, "It's very fabulous." It was not very fabulous. It had no closet. It was in a basement. It was all I could find. And still Lorna helped me move.

Lorna took me in when I was homeless and rude. Her putting me on notice was the best thing she could have done for me. When she kicked me out, that's when I started my own consulting business because I had to pay rent and make my car payment and eat. And here's a funny coda to the story. Two or three months after I moved into my closetless basement with no tub—where you had to walk into the bathroom sideways—my friend, with whom I'd lived when I first moved to DC, told me she needed a place for a month or two. She ended up staying six months.

Toward the end of my stay with Lorna, I really started hustling. Nothing lights a fire like not knowing where you're going to sleep in a few weeks. So I got a meeting at NBC. I was talking with an executive—it was an interview-type scenario—and he asked, "What would you bring?" And I was thinking, *I was just a national press secretary on a major campaign—what do you mean, what would I bring?* Even so, we had a good conversation. He was like, "I like you; you have good energy." Then an assistant came in and handed him a sheet of paper. All of a sudden, he said, "I'm so sorry. I have to end this meeting." We stood up and walked out, and there was Corey Lewandowski sitting there, and they were basically feeding him grapes; he had just left the Trump campaign and every network was trying to get him.

Okay, so I went over to CNN. It was the same thing: "So, what do you bring?" *Why does everyone keep asking me what I bring?!* It felt bratty to say, *I've already been on TV many dozens of times, and I was the national press secretary for a freaking headline campaign!* That should have been self-evident. But apparently it was not. After these meetings, people were telling me, "You need an agent." I made it my mission to get one. I had a couple of phone calls. On my first one, with a person who came highly recommended, I heard, "Honestly, I don't think you're palatable enough for cable television." I had to wonder: Then why exactly had she agreed to talk to me? In retrospect, I think she was taking the meeting out of courtesy to folks who'd recommended me.

Did she mean I was too Black, too bald, too big? Too loud, too proud, too radical? I don't know. I tried not to take it hard, but I had been looking forward to talking to an agent who could help me figure out what I was doing wrong and tweak my strategy so I could get a job. So I talked to another agent. This one said I needed voice lessons. I asked why. She told me, "You don't sound like what folks are used to listening to on TV." In other words, I didn't sound like a white woman.

After being knocked down a few times, I didn't want to talk to any more agents for a while. But then I picked myself up. I wasn't going to take no for an answer. I was going to get myself a TV contract, agent or not. This is easier said than done. (Most people in the TV biz will not talk to you directly; they want to speak with your agent. Same goes in the book biz, by the way.) So you know how

I started? Good ol' Google. I started typing in searches like "talent person CNN." That's how I found the name Amy Entelis. She is the executive VP for talent and content development for CNN Worldwide. In other words, a BFD. I knew I couldn't just call her up. So the gears in my head started turning. *Who do I know who might know her? How am I going to get in front of her?*

The same day that I did this googling, Jake Tapper was having a party to celebrate the beginning of his show in DC, and I got an invite. I wasn't in the mood, but I rallied. As I arrived (late) and got out of my Uber, I saw Amy Entelis on the sidewalk! Thank God for the internet. She was standing with Tammy Haddad—an OG communications star in DC. Everyone knows Tammy; she's super gregarious and has a big personality; she's got an awesome gray swoop of hair. So I said, "Hey, Tammy!" "Oh, Symone! So good to see you!" Then Tammy came through for me big-time. "Amy, let me introduce you—you guys need to just hire Symone!" I owed Tammy favors for life at this point, but I tried to play it cool. We chatted for a moment, and then Amy Entelis gave me her card and was whisked away in a car. Just remember, you never know when the connection will come, so always network and always remember: one day the meeting is going to go well, even if they've all been bad, maybe even very bad, maybe even for a very long time.

A few weeks later, I got invited to a meeting with

Rebecca Kutler at CNN. She asked me about working on Bernie's campaign, asked my thoughts on the election at that point, seemed to actually care about my opinions and my input rather than asking flippant questions like "What do you bring?" All the same, I tried not to get too excited. Afterward, I didn't hear anything. Two weeks later, I followed up, and I got another meeting on the schedule. I sat down with Rebecca again and got ready for a debate. I started off, "Let me just say—" She cut me off. "Well, Symone, we'd like to offer you a contract." Well! Okay! So that's how I ended up with my regular spot on CNN. I appeared on every single show on CNN at some point—*The Lead with Jake Tapper*, *New Day*, *CNN Newsroom*, you name it.

PIECE OF ADVICE

YOU DON'T HAVE TO LISTEN TO NO, BUT YOU DO HAVE TO LISTEN

One thing about pushing for change, especially if you are working in politics or acting as a spokesperson or a public figure, is that you have to have a tough skin. You might not have to listen when someone tells you no, but you can't just ignore everything else they might say! Try to think of people's responses to you as feedback first, rather than insults. Make it your first assumption that what you're hearing is constructive criticism. It's also good to be self-aware and recognize areas for your own self-improvement. You know deep down if you did a bad job or you said something off. We live in a culture where folks are overly sensitive in many respects, to the point where constructive criticism and feedback people really do need is viewed as an attack—the response is often: "They're just trying to silence me! They want to keep my voice from being heard!" You might need to take a chill pill! Sometimes I have to remember to take one too; we all get a little sensitive! Once, I was on the phone with someone talking about my latest appearance on a Sunday show. They said, "I saw the show and you were off your game." I got very defensive, because the delivery was rude, and responded, "NO, I WAS NOT! Were YOU on the Sunday show today?" This person said my voice was raspy, and two to three of my points did not come across clearly. I said, "Well, I was tired! I'd been on a plane and traveling all week!" That may have been true, but that doesn't mean I wasn't off my game. Then I got off the phone, and an hour later I admitted two things: One, I was not 100; I was 75 percent. And two, I was a little too defensive and should take some constructive criticism.

I like to think I was doing my part to speak truth to power while I was on CNN. While speaking that truth though, one thing became very clear to me: media consumption should be a class taught on every single college campus in America. Contrary to what you read on Twitter, America has not turned off the television. So, it's important from two sides: one, because now we're in this crazy world of manufactured news and many people aren't discerning enough about the things they read, hear, and see. We have outsourced our critical thinking where the news is concerned to the internet. Secondly, given the ESPN style of cable news, many people don't know the difference between a commentator, correspondent, and reporter. I am not a reporter and I do not have a journalism degree. I was paid to appear on television to give commentary from a particular perspective. I like to think of political commentators as subject matter specialists in politics for cable news (some better than others). If a young person thinks they want to get involved in the news media, they need to know that they have to put in real work and develop an expertise, whether it's in a subject area or a discipline. They need to know who's doing the work behind the scenes, making the proverbial trains run on time. I would love to have a sort of boot camp, a series of gatherings, where young women, especially women of color, who are interested in news and politics take classes to really crystalize what their goals are and how they will achieve them. Because being a commentator is not all about sitting pretty on TV. And to get past all the nos you're going to hear from people, you have to be prepared and know your stuff.

Nowadays, on the Biden campaign, I've learned yet again that it's important to be prepared—no, *over*prepared. I'm going to do the homework because that's who I am. I stay up late and I get up mad early and I'm constantly reading: online, in the news, on social media. I'm looking over research, and frankly, I could be doing more. You know everybody says, "You've got as many hours a day as Beyoncé." I could always be doing more, but I try to prepare for all contingencies; I study up on whatever they could possibly throw at me. When I was working for CNN, I got comfortable with the idea that I would show up, and someone would tell me these are the topics, and I could prepare myself to discuss those things. I was a little rusty when I was just getting started on campaign work again. (Recall my earlier story about getting caught flat-footed when someone asked me whether the crime bill Biden supported in the 1990s resulted in mass incarceration . . . I wasn't prepared for the conversation. I looked a mess and I looked crazy.) In fact, this challenge is exactly why I felt like I needed to go on the campaign trail again. I started feeling complacent, where I didn't feel like I was contributing as much as I could. I needed to push myself—and also I wanted to get out there and help save the damn republic.

As I got my feet under me at CNN, I chatted a lot with

Roland Martin, Hilary Rosen, and Donna Brazile to get a sense of what I should be doing. They'd all been on TV for a long time, and I valued their advice. I'd literally follow Roland around—I had just started at CNN and he'd tell me when he would be done with a meeting, so I'd go and find him and I'd hold his briefcase and ask him TV questions. But I knew that eventually I wanted to be more than just a commentator, which led me back to campaign work. In the meantime, being on the shows was a hugely valuable experience that I am sure I would sign up for again. However, I don't want anybody to be an "aspiring commentator," and let me tell you why. I was never an aspiring commentator. It was an add-on, a bonus, and a pretty dope one. But when people literally come up to me and say, "How do I become a CNN commentator?" it's more than a little irritating. I want people to aspire to be experts in their field, so they then have the ability to commentate. That's what they should be aspiring to.

When people ask, "How can I be a commentator?" I ask them, "What are you interested in?" "Well, I want to do political commentating," I often hear. Well, what do you do in politics that you are an expert in? As for me, I am an expert communicator. Which I came to be after a lot of hard work as an advocate for juvenile justice, and then as a campaign spokesperson. I'm not an expert commentator; there's more to me than that. There are some people in politics, that's their game, just being a commentator—mmkay. Look, if you're going to be a speaker, you have to be speaking on behalf of something; you have to have a reason for people to trust your interpretation of things or care about your opinion. You need to build a case for yourself as a public persona.

As I mentioned before the group of women who call themselves the Colored Girls: Donna Brazile, Yolanda Caraway, Leah Daughtry, Minyon Moore. These women climbed, fought, worked their tails off to get to incredible positions of power in politics, and they set the foundation for people like me. There's no doubt in my mind that I could not and would not be where I am today if it weren't for them. For the most part, they were working and continue to work as operatives and advisors and such behind the scenes. Except for Donna, who is a commentator, people for the most part literally didn't and don't know these Black women existed. They had to do the work behind the scenes so that young upstarts like me can be out front. Some people might think that there weren't lots of Black women involved in politics at a national level and then—boom—we have a Black woman running to be the Democratic nominee, Black women campaign managers, a Black girl serving as an advisor for Joe Biden. Black women are suddenly popping out in a way that we never have before.

I want to be clear: we have always been here. But in reality, there are lots of Black women in national politics who are making the trains run, who are responsible for executing, who are the reason policies are getting passed and statements are going out and money is being put in places where it really matters and can help communities. But sometimes they aren't visible. We aren't often the press secretaries, the campaign managers, the chief spokespeople, the operatives that the press corps loves to focus on. I think the media and the larger political apparatus have awoken to the power and prowess of Black women. But we are still fighting to be seen in politics, just like the next woman of color in another field that was long closed to us. I am still fighting for the ability to show up every day and not have someone in the press label me, not have the press or even the people, voters, folks, place a burden on my shoulder that I'm not responsible for, or ask me to deliver on something I can't execute.

I've worked really hard my entire career to be the communications person, or the commentator, or the political person, that is also Black. Not the Black commentator, not the Black press person, not the Black political person. Because, yes, I can talk to you, I can keep you woke, we can talk about criminal justice reform, I can tell you why Black lives matter, I can pontificate on those issues, I can be helpful when it comes to crime and justice. I can also talk to you about trade and the economy. Let's talk about NAFTA or trade relations with China or what we should do to engage Iran. I work really hard not to put limits on myself. By not putting limits on myself, I refuse to allow the world to put limits on me. You shouldn't either.

8
THE MOMENT IS NOW

Eventually, you will find yourself in a place where YOU can say no, because you have more experience and more choices and, yes, more power. When you've prepared your best, when you're out there doing the hard work that revolutionary change requires, acting as an accomplice on behalf of others, when you've tested your own limits, and picked yourself up after a couple of hard knocks and learned from them, it's time to jump. Be ruthless in demanding what you want, and what you know you're worth. Be unafraid, and take a leap toward where you want to end up.

At the beginning of 2019, I was preparing to begin my fellowship at the Center for the Political Future at USC, consulting, and still appearing every now and then on cable news. One afternoon, I was on CNN and the topic that day was the road to 2020 and the election. As I sat on the panel, it hit me: I really wanted to be on the campaign trail. I knew it would be hard and often unglamorous; I knew that people were going to put me through the wringer no matter which candidate's team I ended up on, and of course afterward. Now, if I am being honest, I didn't realize it'd be as hard as it turned out to be. Whew. But I knew I didn't want to spend this entire election season pontificating on a panel about the work other people were doing. *I* wanted to do the work. I wanted to be a part of taking down Donald Trump, a part of moving this country forward. There's not going to be another election cycle like this for a long time. No matter what happens, this one is going down in the history books. This was my moment to help make a difference.

In the spring of 2019, I spoke with many candidates pursuing the Democratic nomination for president. And let me remind you that in 2019 there were scores of people out there who were angling to try to be the nominee: twenty-six at one point. The weirder part was that at this point in my career, I knew many of them personally. A little different from my first rodeo in presidential politics! I'd gotten to know Kirsten Gillibrand really well over the previous few years after I interviewed her for a Crooked Media podcast. I had also developed a good relationship with Cory Booker, another genuine friendship. I'm not close with Senator Kamala Harris, but her sister, Maya, is like a big sister to me. I often have asked Maya for not just career advice but life advice too, so you could imagine the day our conversation went from me asking her thoughts on this guy who I was dating, and then the conversation switched to "Do you want to be on our team?"

Elizabeth Warren was another person I spoke with. When I was invited to be a fellow at the Harvard Institute of Politics in Spring of 2018, Elizabeth Warren called to congratulate me, as she does for all of the fellows. (She used to teach at Harvard and is often involved with the IOP.) That phone call was actually hilarious: I was waiting on a member of Congress who was calling me back after we got cut off abruptly. The phone rang, and it said "Unknown." I figured it was this person, and I answered the phone saying, "Hey . . . so . . ." and started talking, and suddenly this voice interrupted me like, "Ah, Symone?" And I was like, "Wait, who is this? Senator Warren?" OOPS.

So how did I finally end up Team Biden, you ask? As the conversations with others progressed, I realized that first and foremost, I wanted to make sure I had a relationship, a rapport, access, autonomy, a voice in creating the candidate's strategy, and, above all else, I wanted to have fun. I didn't want to go somewhere I would be miserable or just be a mouthpiece; I didn't want to come onto a campaign and just be a spokesperson. I wanted to do strategy work because I wanted to add to my skill set, and I also wanted to challenge myself with something more, with contributing to the ideas and the message of the campaign in a deeper way.

Of course, everyone knows who Vice President Biden is, but honestly, I did not think that working on the Biden campaign was an option for me. One, because I didn't know Vice President Biden. I wasn't a part of his very big and historic orbit of trusted people. Two, I wasn't sure that I would be able to do the kind of strategy work I most wanted to do since he has such a plethora of people to choose from, people who are close to him and have been for a long time. And three, I thought, *I'm sure they've got a hundred people waiting in line to speak to them. And I've got too much going on to wait in line to speak to somebody.* (Remember my earlier advice about not waiting in line?)

So I didn't know Biden before, and I didn't know many people in his world. But when they called me, of course I was more than happy to speak with his team. You always take the call, ladies and gentlemen!

The first time I met Vice President Biden, our meeting was only supposed to be thirty to forty minutes. I ended up staying two hours. We had a really enthralling conversation, and just connected. I liked him. I *really* liked him. I liked his wife, Dr. Biden, very much too. Every time he spoke about his vision for the campaign, it resonated with me. After many more conversations with more than a few people, I decided this was where I wanted to be: on a campaign where I could help shape the strategy, really help build the system, and work for a person I genuinely admire and respect. At the end of the day, I decided this was the place I needed to be, where I could be the most effective and where I could really be helpful and where I could grow personally and professionally.

But it was definitely a leap. If I had gone to work for Senator Warren or Senator Booker or Senator Gillibrand, I would have had the foundation of a solid relationship with my principal already set. It would have been comfortable for me. I wanted to make myself a little uncomfortable—to stretch and push myself. The next thing that happened certainly was uncomfortable—it got leaked that I joined the Biden campaign. We were a few days out from when we were going to announce, and reporters were calling me, "We hear that you're on the Biden campaign." I wasn't answering; they were leaving messages or sending text messages. They were emailing. I was like, *What is this? Who did this?* At this point there were only about five people who knew I'd made up my mind. I still had to get in touch with all the other people I'd been talking to and let them know about my decision; I wanted to keep my relationships intact. And so I was on a plane coming back from LA, because I was in the midst of a fellowship at the USC Dornsife Center for the Political Future with Bob Shrum (who advised Edward Kennedy, Joe Biden, John Glenn, and Barbara Mikulski during Senate campaigns, and John Kerry and Al Gore when they ran for president). As I was boarding a flight the Biden comms team told me they had to get out in front of it, so the story was dropping tomorrow. *Uh-oh. Okay. I've got to do my notification calls and emails.*

PIECE OF ADVICE

WHEN YOU FIND YOU'RE THE ONE WHO'S GOT TO TELL SOMEONE NO, DO IT WITH CLASS

Being told time and again, "Be nice, stay in line, know your place, wait your turn, don't make a scene," and all that other bullshit can make certain habits of mind take root even when you are actively working against conforming to those pressures. Women especially are expected to acquiesce to the needs and desires of others, so much so that we sometimes sacrifice what's best for ourselves. Even if we don't cave to the pressure to do this, there's often still a feeling of guilt that's left rattling around in our heads. This can sometimes turn into or manifest as a need-to-please complex. I know because I've got the people-pleaser complex to a degree myself. To combat it we have to learn to trust our instincts, and also to treat people well, with the long-term in mind, even when it's challenging in the moment.

I knew it would be a difficult moment when I had to tell people I considered friends that I'd decided to support someone else. I don't like to disappoint people, so these notification calls were hard for me. And some people I didn't get a chance to call because I waited too long, and the timeline for the announcement got moved up, and I had to get on a plane. And so some folks I had to just text, and some people I emailed, and some people I called. I'm not saying I handled it all perfectly. It was especially hard because these are people that I like, love, and respect, and who have poured their time and efforts into mentoring me. And you know, it's no small thing for somebody to mount a run for president and ask you to be on their team. I didn't want to let anybody down. I never wanted anybody to think that I was doing something against them. But at the end of the day, I had to make a decision for myself. And maybe some people were pissed off or hurt or upset, but I've come to the point where I'm

okay with somebody being mad at me if I know
I'm doing the right thing for me, and it's what
I really want to do. So I made my notification
calls and went to bed, and I woke up the next
day and, boom, the story was out there.

So that's the short story of how I landed on the Biden campaign. And now that I'm here, I've been doing my part in working to restore the soul of our nation, rebuild the backbone of America, and unite the country. Whatever issue one could think of has become a headline in this election—abortion rights, health care, reforming the justice system, improving education for everyone, tackling income inequality, infrastructure, Trump's disastrous foreign policy. But it's not just that it's my job to stay out in front of these issues, it is also that I care deeply about them. I also am very devoted to getting young people engaged in the political process. We need to find a way to speak on the issues that engages as many factions of the Democratic Party as we can, and that's no easy task. We need everyone on board to get Trump out of the White House: millennials, Blue Dogs, boomers, lifetime residents of Hillaryland, rural residents, Dreamers, Hollywood stars, white women, Asian, brown, and Black men, old people—everyone. The Democratic apparatus can and must communicate across the Democratic Party factions more effectively. We need to move forward as a more collective whole. I don't believe in ideological purity; I don't believe in ostracizing and excluding people. We have all got to work together if we're going to get shit done. This is a historical, pivotal moment in our nation's history, and we have to come together and act NOW.

When I had my fellowship at Harvard's Institute of Politics, I talked to young, incredibly bright, and engaged people about what they wanted most from the Democratic Party. They said they wanted a voice, one that would be heard and acknowledged by the apparatus. To that I said: "Sure, the American people, you included, should be involved in the messaging of the Democratic Party. But we still need a leader." So, I challenged them, "What does that leader need to look like? Who does that leader need to be?" The answer I heard was that they wanted somebody who is authentic, with real stories and a real heart. Someone who has a vision, who is looking to create an America that includes all the factions (a difficult task that requires a true visionary). We want someone with a diverse team so that the American people can see themselves in the president's entourage. And we need someone who truly cares—about the people of this country, and the future of this nation. The American people want to see more folks who honestly, authentically, and genuinely give a damn about our democracy. And the only way for this to happen is for a candidate to *communicate* their authenticity effectively.

That's where I come in to play my part. I believe that Joe Biden has the qualities we need in our next president, and I'm out there just trying to contribute what and where I can to get him elected. I am just an operative, like others who are working their tails off this cycle. I am just an aide trying to do the best job for the candidate that I signed on to help; I am somebody who wants to get the VP across the finish line. Everything that I do on this campaign is in service of that. But I'm also somebody who knows exactly who I am. I don't have to be the Black political person; I'm a political person. Yes, I'm Black; yes, I'm a millennial; yes, I'm a woman, and I bring my whole self to work every day.

To be clear, I'm up for the job, for the hard work and the second-guesses and the shade. In some respects, it's like being a broker: you can take credit when you advise someone to take stock in a company that skyrockets, but then you also have to take responsibility for one that tanks. You gotta embrace it all.

Moving forward, instead of ragging on young people and the young at heart, the country needs to embrace us. Instead of downplaying our contributions, people need to recognize our power, especially now that we're more ready than ever to wield it. Millennials are generally defined as those people born between 1980 and 1997. We are the children of the baby boomer generation, the largest generation in the history of America, and we compose a third (!) of the world's population. In numbers alone, we are a force to be reckoned with. However, this is only one of many reasons why polling and engaging young people are so important. Our opinions matter because we are the up-and-coming businessmen and -women, entrepreneurs; we are college students, mothers, and fathers; we are also the first generation that came of age in the technology era.

We are vital to the future and the current success of politics as a whole. Young people are quite literally the future of Democratic and Republican thought, and if the political powers that be do not engage us effectively, the apparatus will cease to function. So, the big question: How can we best be engaged?

Any meaningful conversation about young people must look at the changes in this faction over time. Before the terrorist attack of 9/11, young people weren't overly engaged. After 9/11, the consciousness around politics grew tremendously, and young people were voting more than ever. Since then, our opinions and priorities have continued to change. In the last five years, we have moved the political conversation to a more progressive place around issues ranging from affirmative action and trade to climate change and health care.

While I was at Harvard I regularly spoke with young people about how to engage other young people in the political area. I dedicated a whole class to it and I invited John Della Volpe, director of polling at IOP and founder of SocialSphere, to join me for that lesson. The IOP's Public

Opinion Project was started by students in 2000 to gauge the opinions of Americans aged eighteen to twenty-nine on national politics in America. Eighteen years later, this poll was still running, producing annual statistics concerning the civic engagement of young Americans. It provides clear evidence of the progressive shift. IOP polling in 2018 found that the portion of young people who feel that immigration helps the country rather than harms it has grown, even in the span of four years, from one-fourth of the young people polled in 2014 to one third in 2018. On gun control, five years ago 49 percent of eighteen- to twenty-nine-year-olds supported stricter laws. Now that number stands at 64 percent. At the same time, young people's identification with the Democratic Party specifically and its beliefs has waned: only 19 percent of young Americans call themselves capitalist, and only 66 percent of young Americans believe the Democratic Party cares about them. Accordingly, the Democratic apparatus is losing its sway with young people, and losing it fast. How, then, can we get them back? Or rather, what can the Democratic Party do to get *us* back?

In speaking to Harvard students and also many other young people across the country, I have been reaffirmed that politics feels tangible for many of us today because of how we've broken through and commanded space since 2016. The change we have seen and the victories we have won are a direct result of our engagement. In the aftermath of the Ferguson uprising, a movement led to an intergenerational coalition of people organizing around the ballot box. Thanks to that work, Wesley Bell, a young, Black leader in criminal justice reform, now heads the same prosecutor's office that once failed to deliver justice to Michael Brown's family. In Wisconsin, Scott Walker's career ended with the election of Democratic Governor Tony Evers and Lieutenant Governor Mandela Barnes and history was made. Mandela is the first African American to be elected lieutenant governor in Wisconsin's history. The people did that work. As we have already discussed, the 2018 midterm elections ushered in a class in Congress that is more diverse in thought, geography, background, and experience and more representative of the country than any other—we, the people, made that happen.

And as 2020 rolls around, I am encouraged by the potential of our progress. This is our moment to reach higher, to show up where we failed to be present before, and to further influence the conversation and trajectory of our country.

I truly do believe that we are at a pivotal moment in our story as a nation. I believe that the history books will review what happens over the course of the next year and a half and that that will literally dictate how life unfolds for the next twenty years. There are lasting implications for what is happening right now. We cannot afford another four years of this type of damage. As it is, it will take another generation and a half to recover from what has happened in the Trump administration thus far. We have to stand up and say this is who we would really like to be, and I and my colleagues need to go out there and make that case to the American people.

That said, as a Black woman, I don't believe anyone should blindly give their support or votes to any one political party or candidate, and no one should expect us to. The life and legacy of one of my idols, Fannie Lou Hamer, teaches us that we have to demand what we are due. Fannie was born in 1917, the last child of twenty (twenty!) born to Ella and James Townsend, who were sharecroppers in Montgomery County, Mississippi. By the age of six she was out in the cotton fields working alongside her siblings and her parents. The Townsend children often ate nothing more than greens with flour gravy or cornmeal with an onion for dinner, and tied rags on their feet when the weather got cold. Despite how hard it was just getting by, Ella and James saw to it that Fannie went to school. She continued her education until the eighth grade, which was rare for Black children (the school "year" for Black children ran only from December to March, so as not to interfere with field work. White children went to school three months more). The fact that she could read and write came as a surprise to the man she married in 1944, Perry Hamer. He put her in charge of keeping records for their own share-cropping work on a plantation in Ruleville, Mississippi.

Fannie and Perry didn't have any biological children of their own, but they adopted two girls; then, in 1961 when Fannie had surgery to remove a benign tumor, she was unwillingly and unknowingly given a hysterectomy—the forced sterilization procedure was so common among Black women in the South at the time that it was called a "Mississippi appendectomy."

The tragedy was a call to action for Hamer, and it planted the seeds for her work as an activist for civil rights and human rights that took root and bore fruit over the rest of her life. In 1962, she went to her first Student Non-violent Coordinating Committee (SNCC) meeting, where she learned that Black people were allowed to vote and immediately volunteered to register at the courthouse the next day. She later said, "I guess if I'd had any sense, I'd a been a little scared. But what was the point of being scared? The only thing the whites could do was kill me, and it seemed like they'd been trying to do that a little bit at a time since I could remember." When she got back to the farm after visiting the courthouse (and being turned away for failing a rigged "literacy test" that asked her to interpret elements of the state constitution), she was fired from her job. In 1963, she went to a training hosted by the Southern Christian Leadership Conference (SCLC), and on the bus ride on the way back, she was arrested at a rest stop when the restaurant refused to serve some members of her group. She was taken to the county jail and beaten to within inches of her life for refusing to say, "Yes, sir," to a police officer.

Fannie Lou Hamer walked with a limp for the rest of her life, but she didn't slow down. She helped form and then joined the Mississippi Freedom Democratic Party, and in 1964 she ran for state Congress. She didn't win, but her campaign speech still echoes: "We are sick and tired of being sick and tired. For so many years, the Negroes have suffered in the state of Mississippi." Also in 1964, she gave a speech before the Democratic National Committee's credentials panel to protest the all-white delegation representing the state of Mississippi (Martin Luther King Jr. also presented at the same event). By the 1968 convention, Hamer was seated as a delegate at the Democratic presidential nominating convention. The next few years she continued her antipoverty and civil rights work, but suffered from bouts of ill health. She died of cancer in 1977, but her legacy as one of the most courageous and powerful orators of the civil rights era endures.

If Hamer can speak out so courageously, with her life at risk, you and I can stand up and say something too. We have to be willing to march into the convention hall and make our case in the face of misogyny, racism, and classism. We have to be willing to actively participate in order to put pressure on the levers of power to bend to our will. Because if we don't, we have the most to lose. If Roe v. Wade is overturned, it is Black women and women of color who will suffer the most. If the current administration and their allies are successful in gutting the Affordable Care Act, it is Black women and women of color who will be locked out of viable health-care options for ourselves and our families. While the wealth gap is already a chasm that deeply separates black and white Americans, it is Black women who are disproportionately affected. Literally, our issues, our lives, are on the ballot.

These are pivotal times in our nation, especially in politics. The pendulum is swinging right now; there is movement and energy—but eventually, this battle will be over. The question becomes: Where will Black women, and marginalized voices of all kinds, sit on the political spectrum when the pendulum comes to rest? Will we have increased the number of Black women in elected offices around the country? Will we be able to claim victory in the form of a more equitable health-care system, economy, and criminal justice system? Will our political prowess finally translate to the financial resources and the power we are due, so that we can continue the work? None of the answers to these questions will come without our active participation. We have to vote, we have to march, we have to protest, we have to organize, we have to support local organizations, we have to leverage our positions to help create a more equitable environment for all of us.

EPILOGUE

Our country is in a dark, strange place. We are keeping children in cages. We are taking away rights that women have held for half a century, after generations of sacrifices by so many to achieve them. We have a president that consorts with our sworn foreign enemies. We are desperate: socially, economically, psychically. We are also more informed, diverse, and determined than we have ever been: as a country and as an electorate. And, perhaps most important, we are pissed as hell.

We're standing at the threshold of a transformation. But in order to achieve it, we need to commit to radical, revolutionary acts. I don't mean lying down in the street or giving speeches to thousands of people. One

way we can begin is by having constructive, uncom-
fortable conversations—in our homes, in our commu-
nities, on the national political stage—about the issues
that matter to us. I'm not talking about having debates
(though I do know a thing or two about prepping for
them: Ugh. Eighteen-hour days in a bunker-like room
eating sandwiches). So instead of debates, let's start hav-
ing constructive, critical conversations. Doing so leaves
space for divergent views. For difference. For questioning.
For innovation and creativity. For change.

Yes, we must question the apparatus. But let's start tak-
ing the next steps too. We must also work to refashion it,
with new materials. We can't simply critique the machine
that makes the Democratic Party or the Republican Party
run; we have to conceptualize ways to change it. Here's
how we can begin. First, if you feel called to represent the
people of this nation, on the most micro or the most macro
levels, DO IT. Don't let the existing conditions of the ap-
paratus deter you. Don't let anyone tell you that someone
"like you" has never done what you are attempting before,
or never served in such a role before. You don't need to
wait your turn. And you sure as hell don't need to apolo-
gize for being the first young person, Black person, Latino
person, non-cis person, differently abled person, to do
something. Second, for too long politicians have focused
on answering the question of what "kind" of campaign we

need to mount or run in order to win. As opposed to who am I and how can I run a campaign that is authentic and representative of who I am and what I believe. Third, (and this is for the Democrats in the room) we need to get more involved in party-wide organizing: when Democratic politicians rise in the ranks of American politics, some develop a sudden amnesia about the down-ballot positions they just held. As a party, we care too much about the big races and not enough about the small ones. Which is crazy because *taps mic* AMERICA'S POLICY IS MADE IN STATE LEGISLATURES! Priming young politicians through small offices is a central pole of the Republican Party tent that the Democrats don't have, or it doesn't seem very sturdy. It's something we can learn from them. If we want to get past the GOP in 2020, we might need to adopt a tactic or two. We can begin with small victories and fill local and statewide positions with folks who really represent their constituencies. Democratic officers need to be representative of the changing times.

As we head into one of the most bizarre presidential elections in history, the Democratic Party is at a crossroads. Some of the most pressing questions remain to be answered: What role will millennials, particularly millennials of color, play in the next chapter of American history? Will "progressives" be able to come together as a coalition and take their place at the table, adding strength to a party that many feel has betrayed them? Will Black women continue to support a party that has often viewed them as an afterthought, and if so, what does their support in 2020 look like? Where does the Democratic Party go from here?

Our institutions are only as strong as the people who support them. The Democratic Party and our democracy as a whole are no different. Communication, I believe, is an art, and where institutions and organizations fail is communication and engagement. How long can a political party truly thrive without the support of the people who make the institution what it is? There is a price to pay for ignoring the will of the people and failing to engage with them. The crossroads we stand at in the Democratic Party specifically and in American politics in general as we approach 2020 speaks to this very problem.

I believe now more than ever that unconventional coalitions and movements are the key to shifting the conversation; they will put us on the right path toward a brighter tomorrow. I know because I've had a front-row seat, participating in events and coalitions that have resulted in actionable policy changes that have improved and will continue to improve lives. Young activists took to the streets from Ferguson to Baton Rouge to ring the alarm on police brutality while simultaneously launching policy and organizing platforms. Young people rose up after the Parkland shootings to demand that we rethink gun control. Young congresswomen of color are rethinking the economy and pushing the government to take action, real action, before climate change wreaks complete havoc on the world as we know it. People all over America right now are doing what they can where they can to save the republic. It is happening.

It may not feel like it every day, but I promise you, we have the power. We can do this. From the office to the classroom, to the ballot box and the strike line, we have the power. Whether you live in a rural community or an urban center, our voices can and do change things. Find your place, ladies and gentlemen. Rise up. This is our country and our participation is mandatory for change. It is our engagement that is the source of the gains we have made and can continue to make in our country toward a more equitable, safe, healthy, and hopeful future for us all.

ACKNOWLEDGMENTS

I never thought I could write a book, so I have to start by thanking the people who made this all possible. Sarah Haugen is not only my editor at HarperCollins, but one of the people who believed I could do this even when I did not. To my amazing agent team at United Talent Agency—Jennifer Campanile, Lia Aponte, Brandi Bowles, and Maddie Landon—thank you for stalking me on email, for your unwavering support, the real talk, and your repeated reminders (I read them). To Shannon O'Neill, the GOAT of all collaborators, who understood my vision, my passion, and my voice—you are now in the family, Shannon!

I am eternally grateful to two real writers and good friends whose encouragement on this journey made all the difference: Cleo Wade and Touré. Cleo's selflessness is humbling and, on the journey of writing this book, she helped me articulate what I needed and gave me the confidence that I knew what I was doing. One evening in New York, Touré reminded me my voice did actually matter and I had something to say—and furthermore, people would want to read it.

To the groupchat that became my cover art focus group, Alyse Newhouse, Maude Okrah, and Kathy Leflore, and to Christopher Huntley, who endured multiple early terrible drafts of my introduction, thank you for lending your eyes and ears and as always for your friendship.

To my partner in crime, Shawn, who forced me to work on this book while on planes, trains, and in automobiles, thank you for not letting up on me. Thank you for reading my edits, telling me when something was terrible, and participating in my voice recording sessions. You are the gift that keeps on giving, my love.

To my mother, my biggest cheerleader, who has never not been in my corner, thank you for supporting me in my development as the independent, outspoken human being that I am. Without you, I probably wouldn't have been interrupting that man on TV, he would not have told me to shut up, and we would not have this book.

Finally, to my students at the Harvard IOP and at USC's Center for the Political Future, please know you all are brilliant, and I am immensely grateful for the symbiotic relationship you each fostered in the classroom. This book is a culmination of the critical thinking conversations we had throughout my fellowship at your respective institutions. Thank you for helping change the world.

ABOUT THE AUTHOR

SYMONE D. SANDERS is a senior advisor for former vice president Joe Biden's 2020 presidential campaign. She also serves as principal of the 360 Group LLC, where she provides strategic communications guidance to organizations, businesses, individuals, campaigns, and candidates and helps clients find sound solutions to tough political and social problems.

Sanders is the former chair of the Coalition of Juvenile Justice Emerging Leaders Committee and former member of the Federal Advisory Committee on Juvenile Justice, where she worked to raise the profile of young voices in the fight for juvenile justice reform and bring millennial perspectives to policy conversations. Sanders is a former CNN political commentator and served as a resident fellow at the Institute of Politics at Harvard's Kennedy School in 2018 and the University of Southern California's Center for the Political Future in 2019.